Business Bullshit

Things They Don't Teach You in Business School

Mike Ross

Business Bullshit – Things They Don't Teach You in Business School

Copyright 2025 – Mike Ross

Paperback Edition ISBN – 978-1-949802-53-5

Published by Black Pawn Press

FIRST EDITION

Dedication

I want to give a special thanks to my mother-in-law, Jean. On my first date with her daughter, she kept me talking about business for so long that I ended up late! Who knew a date could turn into a business meeting? Thanks for the unforgettable start to my journey—and for inspiring the title of my new book, *Business Bullshit!*

Preface

This book is the result of over 30 years of entrepreneurship. I've built multiple companies from the ground up, navigated successes, survived failures, and learned more than I ever thought possible about what works—and what doesn't. My goal here is simple: to save you time, money, and minimize mistakes by sharing the lessons I wish someone had told me when I was starting out.

Here's the truth most business books won't tell you: entrepreneurship isn't all innovation, freedom, and Instagram-worthy wins. Sure, those moments exist, but what no one prepares you for is the other side. The bureaucratic nonsense, dealing with banks, attorneys, vendors, employees, the confusing jargon, the relentless red tape, and the sheer absurdity of some of the situations you'll face. That's the *business bullshit*—the stuff no one talks about, but every entrepreneur ends up dealing with.

This book is your guide to navigating that bullshit. It's not filled with fluff or magic formulas. This is the raw, unfiltered truth about what it really takes to run a business in the real world—and how to handle the curveballs you never saw coming.

Whether you're just starting out or you've been in the game for years, this book will give you practical advice, hard-earned insights, and a few laughs along the way. My hope is that by the time you're done reading, you'll feel more confident, more prepared, and a hell of a lot less alone in the chaos of entrepreneurship.

Welcome to *Business Bullshit*. If you're holding this book, chances are you've run into the brick walls, headaches, and outright madness that come with building and running a business. Let me tell you—you're not alone.

So, buckle up. This isn't going to be another sugar-coated business fairy tale. This is *Business Bullshit*. Let's get to it.

In *Business Bullshit,* I'll walk you through the most common (and some not-so-common) challenges that entrepreneurs face, from dealing with impossible regulations to managing unmotivated teams, from decoding corporate jargon to handling the emotional rollercoaster of ownership. More importantly, I'll show you how to cut through the noise, find clarity, and move forward with confidence.

This book is not just a guide—it's a Conversation---it's Problem Solving---its Electrifying! I'm going to be brutally honest about the struggles and just as transparent about the solutions. My hope is that by the time you turn the last page, you'll feel empowered, energized, equipped, and ready to face whatever the business world throws your way.

You will read throughout my book the three most important parts of running a *successful* business:

1. Cash Flow

2. Happy Customers

3. Happy Employees

Contents

Chapter 1: So Much for Protection

You did it. You jumped through all the hoops, paid all the fees, and now you've got those magic letters— "LLC" or "Inc."—stamped next to your business name. It feels like you just leveled up, doesn't it? You're not just some scrappy hustler anymore; you're *legit*. Official. And best of all, you've got that sweet, sweet protection. Your house? Safe. Your car? Untouchable. Your embarrassingly large collection of vintage action figures? Still, yours to admire in secret. That's the whole point of setting up a corporation or LLC, right? You draw a line in the sand between your business and personal life. You're untouchable... or at least, that's what you've been told.

The Illusion of Protection

Here's the harsh truth: that shiny corporate veil you're so proud of? It's not as impenetrable as you think. Sure, in theory, your personal assets are separate from your business. That's the promise you bought into. But in practice? It's more like a curtain than a wall. If someone's mad enough—or desperate enough—they'll find a way to pull that curtain back. And suddenly, the personal fortress you thought you built looks more like a house of cards.

Why You're Not as Protected as You Think

Let's break down why your "ironclad" protection might actually be a rusty screen door:

1. Piercing the Corporate Veil

Ah, the dreaded "piercing the corporate veil." Sounds like something out of a medieval fantasy novel, doesn't it? But in the real world, it's just a fancy way of saying a court can decide your LLC or corporation isn't good enough to shield you. Here's how they can make that happen:

- Commingling Funds: If you're using your business account to pay for personal expenses—or vice versa—you're basically begging someone to take a sledgehammer to your corporate veil.
- Fraud or Misrepresentation: If you've been shady, sloppy, or downright negligent, don't be surprised when someone tries to hold you personally responsible.

2. Personal Guarantees

Remember that lease you signed or that loan you took out where they made you sign a personal guarantee? Yeah, that's like handing someone a spare key to your personal assets. If your business can't pay, guess who's on the hook? You.

3. Lawsuits Against You Personally

This is the big one most people don't realize. Just because you have an LLC or corporation doesn't mean someone can't sue *you* personally. Customers, employees, and contractors they'll come for you if they think it'll lead to a bigger payday.

What to Do When the Envelope Lands on Your Desk

Let's say the worst happens: you get served with a lawsuit. That thick envelope lands on your desk and your stomach drops. Now what?

1. Lawyer Up—and Make It a Damn Good Lawyer specializing in your profession

This isn't the time to cut corners. You need a heavy hitter—a specialized attorney who knows your industry inside and out. If you're running a construction company, hire a lawyer who eats, sleeps, and breathes construction law. Don't just take their word for it—grill them with questions. Make sure they know their stuff because your livelihood depends on it.

2. Stay Calm—Judgment Takes Time

Just because someone sues you doesn't mean they'll win. Lawsuits take time—discovery, depositions, negotiations, maybe even a trial. Until a judgment is handed down, you're not guilty of anything. Stay calm, follow your lawyer's advice, and don't let the stress derail your business.

Proactive Steps to Protect Yourself

Look, the best way to handle this kind of business bullshit is to avoid it in the first place. Here's how:

1. Create a Family and Company Trust

Move your personal assets into a trust. This separates your wealth from your name, making it a hell of a lot harder for creditors or lawsuits to come after your house, savings, or anything else you hold dear.

2. Form an LLC for Each Project

Yeah, it sounds like overkill, but creating separate LLCs for each major project is one of the smartest moves you can make. If one job goes sideways, it won't drag your entire company down with it. Compartmentalize your risk.

3. Keep Finances Clean and Separate

This one's non-negotiable. Never mix personal and business money. Pay yourself a salary, keep detailed records, and treat your business like the separate entity it's supposed to be.

4. Avoid Personal Guarantees When Possible

Sometimes you can't avoid signing a personal guarantee—it's just the cost of doing business. But when you can, push back. Negotiate terms that keep your personal assets out of the equation.

5. Hire one lawyer for general law, such as entity formation and to ask general law questions. Have the other lawyer when a lawsuit arrives that specializes in your profession or for what area you are being sued.

The Bottom Line

Here's the deal: the corporate veil isn't a magic cloak. It's more like a shield—and shields can crack if you don't take care of them. You've got to be proactive. Move your assets into trusts, keep your finances squeaky clean, compartmentalize your risk, and for the love of all things holy, hire a lawyer who knows their craft. Because at the end of the day, protecting yourself isn't just about filing paperwork—it's about being smarter, sharper, and two steps ahead of the bullshit.

*"Nothing can be made except by makers, nothing can be managed except by managers. Money cannot make anything, and money cannot manage anything." Two classes of people lose money; those who are too weak to guard what they have; those who win money by trick. They both lose in the end." - **Henry Ford***

Chapter 2: No Sales = No Company

Sales isn't just a department, it's the life blood of your business. And yet, for some reason, it's often treated as an afterthought. I've seen founders obsess over product development, burn through cash on marketing campaigns, and spend months writing the perfect business plan, all while ignoring the single most important question: Who's going to buy this, and how are we going to sell it to them?

If I had a dollar for every time I heard an entrepreneur say, "We're going to focus on sales later," I wouldn't need to sell anything myself. The hard truth is this: without sales, your company doesn't exist. You can have the most innovative product, the slickest branding, and a killer mission statement, but if no one's buying what you're selling, you're dead in the water.

In this chapter, I'm going to break down the bullshit around sales and show you why it's not just a necessary evil—it's the foundation of everything you do. Whether you're a natural-born closer or someone who breaks out in a cold sweat at the thought of pitching, sales is a skill you can't afford to ignore.

The Bullshit Excuses for Avoiding Sales

Let's start with the excuses, because I've heard them all—and, if I'm honest, I've used a few of them myself:

1. **"I'm not a salesperson."**

   Newsflash: If you're a CEO or entrepreneur, you are a salesperson. Whether you're pitching to investors, negotiating with vendors, or convincing your team to buy into your vision, you're selling every single day. The sooner you accept that, the better.

2. **"Our product sells itself."**

   This is one of the biggest lies in business. No product sells itself. Even Apple, with all its brand loyalty and cult-like following, invests billions in sales and marketing. If you think your product is the exception, you're in for a rude awakening.

3. **"We'll focus on sales after we finish [insert excuse here]."**

   Whether it's finalizing your prototype, building your website, or hiring your team, there's always going to be something that feels more urgent than sales. But here's the thing: sales can't wait. If you're not selling, you're not learning, and if you're not learning, your business isn't growing.

4. **"I don't want to be pushy."**

   No one likes a pushy salesperson, but that doesn't mean you get to avoid sales altogether. Selling isn't about manipulation—it's about helping people solve a problem. If you believe in what you're selling, it's not pushy; it's necessary.

Sales Is a Process, Not Magic

One of the biggest misconceptions about sales is that it's all about charisma—that you either have it or you don't. But the truth is, sales isn't magic; it's a process. And like any process, it can be learned, improved, and scaled.

Here's what the sales process generally looks like:

1. **Prospecting:**

   This is where it all begins—finding the people who might be interested in what you're selling. Whether it's cold calls, LinkedIn messages, or networking events, prospecting is about building a pipeline of potential customers. It's not glamorous, but it's essential.

2. **Qualifying:**

   Not everyone in your pipeline is a good fit for your product or service. Qualifying is about identifying the people who actually need what you're selling and have the budget to buy it. Spend your time on the right leads, not just any leads.

3. **Pitching:**

   This is where you get to shine—or stumble. A good pitch isn't about talking nonstop; it's about listening, understanding your prospect's pain points, and showing them how your product solves their problem. Remember: it's not about you; it's about them.

4. **Handling Objections:**

   No sale is ever straightforward. You'll hear every excuse in the book—"It's too expensive," "We're not ready yet," "We're going with a competitor." The key is to address these objections calmly and confidently, showing why your solution is worth it.

5. **Closing the Deal:**

   This is the moment of truth. Closing isn't about tricking

someone into saying yes; it's about creating a win-win situation where both parties feel good about the decision. And once the deal is closed, don't forget to follow up and nurture the relationship.

The Bullshit You'll Encounter in Sales

Sales isn't just hard work, it's full of bullshit. Here's what you can expect:

1. **The "Interested" Prospect Who Never Buys:**

   They'll nod along enthusiastically, tell you how much they love your product, and then ghost you when it's time to sign the contract. These tire-kickers will waste your time if you let them, so learn to spot the difference between genuine interest and empty enthusiasm.

2. **The Price Haggler:**

   No matter how fairly you price your product, there will always be someone who tries to nickel-and-dime you. Stand your ground. If you cave too easily, you'll devalue your product—and yourself.

3. **The Competitor Comparison Game:**

   "Why should I buy from you when [competitor] offers the same thing for less?" This is where you need to know your value proposition inside and out. What makes you different? Why are you worth the premium? If you can't answer that, you've already lost.

4. **Rejection—Lots of It:**

Sales is a numbers game, and rejection is part of the process. You'll hear "no" more times than you can count, but every "no" gets you closer to a "yes." The key is not to take it personally.

Lessons I've Learned the Hard Way

If I could go back and give my younger self some advice about sales, here's what I'd say:

1. **Start Selling Early:**

Don't wait until your product is perfect. Start selling as soon as you have something to offer, even if it's just an idea. Early sales will give you valuable feedback and help you refine your product.

2. **Invest in Relationships:**

Sales isn't just about closing deals; it's about building trust. The best salespeople aren't the ones who make the most noise—they're the ones who genuinely care about their customers.

3. **Focus on Value, Not Features:**

People don't buy products; they buy solutions. Instead of listing features, show your prospects how your product will make their life easier, cheaper, or better.

4. **Embrace the Grind:**

Sales is hard, repetitive, and often thankless work. But it's also the most important thing you'll do for your business. Embrace the grind, and don't give up.

The Pressure Is Real

I'll never forget one brutal month early in my business. Sales were down, bills were stacking up, and payroll was looming like a storm cloud over my head.

The pressure to sell isn't just about keeping your business afloat— it's personal. It's about supporting your family, paying your employees, and maintaining your reputation. It's about not looking like a total failure. That kind of weight can crush you if you let it.

But here's the thing: pressure has a way of forcing you to get creative. When your back's against the wall, you start thinking outside the box. And sometimes, those moments of desperation lead to breakthroughs you never saw coming.

My Early Sales Screw-Ups

Nobody starts out as a sales expert. I sure didn't. I learned how to sell the hard way—by making every mistake in the book. Here are a few gems from my greatest hits of failure:

1. Talking Too Much

When I first started, I thought selling meant talking... a lot. I'd launch into full-blown monologues about every feature, benefit, and detail of whatever I was selling, thinking the more I said, the more convincing I'd be.

Turns out, people don't want a lecture. They want a conversation. They want to feel heard, not bombarded. They want to see what you can bring to the table that will give thema better life—better investment.

Lesson learned: Shut up and listen. The best salespeople ask great questions and let the customer do most of the talking.

2. Chasing the Wrong Customers

My entire staff MUST know who our IDEAL customer is at all times— in everything we do. In the beginning, I thought every potential customer was worth chasing. I'd bend over backward to accommodate people who clearly weren't a good fit, just to make a sale. The result? I ended up with customers who were a nightmare—constant complaints, unreasonable demands, and zero loyalty.

Lesson learned: Not every customer is worth your time. Focus on the people who actually need what you're offering and who won't make your life miserable.

3. Undervaluing My Offer

I was terrified of scaring people off with my prices. So, I'd discount everything, throw in freebies, and basically bend over backward to make the sale. But all I was doing was selling myself short—and undervaluing my business.

Lesson learned: If you don't believe in the value of what you're selling, no one else will either. Price confidently and stand by your worth.

The Sales Rollercoaster

Sales is a ride, and it's not for the faint of heart. One day, you're on top of the world, closing deals left and right. The next, your inbox is a ghost town, and you're wondering if everyone decided to boycott your business.

I've had days where I felt like an unstoppable sales machine—like the time I closed a deal worth more than my entire previous month's revenue. And I've had days where I couldn't sell water to a guy stranded in the desert.

The trick is not to let the highs or the lows mess with your head. Celebrate the wins, learn from the losses, and keep moving forward.

How I Handle the Pressure of Sales

Sales pressure is real, and it's not going anywhere. But over the years, I've learned how to manage it without losing my mind (most of the time). Here's what works for me:

1. Focus on Relationships, Not Just Transactions

When you're desperate for sales, it's tempting to rush the process. But people can smell desperation a mile away, and it's not a good look.

The best sales come from building real relationships. Take the time to understand your customers, offer value, and earn their trust. When people feel like you actually care, they're more likely to buy—and keep coming back.

2. Have a Plan

Flying by the seat of your pants in sales is a recipe for disaster. I set monthly, weekly, and even daily sales goals to keep myself focused. And if I'm not hitting those goals? I tweak my approach instead of freaking out.

3. Diversify Your Revenue Streams

Relying on one customer, product, or market is asking for trouble. If that one thing goes south, you're screwed. That's why I've worked hard to diversify—offering different products, targeting various types of customers, and exploring multiple sales channels.

4. Don't Take Rejection Personally

Rejection is part of the game, and it still stings every time. But I've learned not to take it personally. A "no" doesn't mean you suck—it just means they're not the right fit, or the timing isn't right.

5. Celebrate the Small Wins

Sales is tough, and it's easy to feel discouraged. That's why I make it a point to celebrate every win, no matter how small. Whether it's landing a new customer, closing a tiny deal, or even just getting a positive email, those little victories keep me going.

Reading Your Potential Customers on the first meeting

1. Ask questions to find out exactly what their needs are.

2. Have they had a previous bad experience with another company?

3. Always ask them for the job once you present them with your proposal. Make them tell you no, as most customers do not feel comfortable saying no.

4. Determine which one of these three things is MOST important to them.
   - Cost
   - Job Specifications(details)
   - Time

The Business Bullshit of Sales

My brother Gary always said this about my daughter Christine. When she hears someone tell her "No" she thinks "Next"

So here's my advice: embrace the grind, focus on building real relationships, and remember that *every "no" brings you closer to a "yes."* Sales will test you, but it'll also teach you resilience, creativity, and the value of persistence.

"Sales aren't just about transactions, but about building relationships, understanding customer needs, and creating value. Effective sales rely on communication, problem-solving, and a focus on helping customers achieve their goals." - **Roli Saxena, Co-Founder of the LinkedIn Women's Network**

Chapter 3: Recognizing and Avoiding Business Scams and Hype

The truth is, avoiding scams and hype is one of the most important skills you'll need as an entrepreneur. Because while business scams are some of the most frustrating kinds of bullshit you'll deal with, they're also some of the most dangerous. They don't just waste your time—they can wreck your reputation, drain your bank account, and set your business back by months or even years.

Some of them are obvious—the Nigerian prince emails of the professional world. But others are harder to spot. They look legit, sound impressive, and prey on your ambition or inexperience. And if you're not careful, you'll find yourself throwing money, time, and energy into something that's either a waste—or a complete scam.

So let's break it down. What are the red flags, the common traps, and the tools you need to keep yourself—and your business—safe?

The Anatomy of a Scam

Business scams come in all shapes and sizes, but they all have one thing in common—they're designed to exploit your trust. Here's how they usually work:

1. **They Appeal to Your Desperation or Ambition.**

   Scammers know that entrepreneurs are hungry. Maybe you're hustling to grow, or maybe you're struggling to survive. Either way, they'll dangle something in front of you that seems like the perfect solution to your problems.

2. **They Overpromise and Under-deliver.**

The hallmark of any scam is the promise of results that sound too good to be true. "Double your revenue in 30 days!" "Guaranteed ROI!" "Zero risk!" Spoiler alert: there's always a catch.

3. **They Pressure You to Act Fast.**

Scammers thrive on urgency. "This opportunity won't last!" "You need to act now!" The faster they can get you to commit, the less time you have to think critically—or do your homework.

4. **They Hide the Fine Print.**

Whether it's through hidden fees, unclear terms, or vague deliverables, scammers rely on ambiguity. If they can keep you in the dark, they can take advantage of you before you realize what's happening.

My First Scam Encounter

Let me take you back to one of my earliest brushes with a scam. I was just starting out and eager to grow my business. One day, I got an email from a "business coach" who promised to teach me the secret to scaling my company. His pitch was slick—he had testimonials, flashy graphics, and even a countdown timer to push me into signing up for his "exclusive" program.

I'll admit it—I got sucked in. I paid the fee (which wasn't cheap) and joined the program, only to realize it was a total joke. The "coaching" was generic advice I could've found on Google for free, and the promised one-on-one sessions? Nonexistent.

It was a hard pill to swallow, but it taught me an important lesson: if something feels off, it probably is.

The Hype Trap

Scams aren't the only thing you need to watch out for. Hype can be just as dangerous.

The business world is full of trends that promise to revolutionize everything. Block Chain! NFTs! AI tools that will run your company while you sleep! And while some of these trends have legitimate value, a lot of them are just noise.

The problem with hype is that it creates a herd mentality. Everyone starts jumping on the bandwagon, and you feel like you have to do the same—or risk getting left behind. But chasing every trend will burn you out faster than you can say "disruption."

How to Spot a Scam (or Hype)

Over the years, I've gotten pretty good at sniffing out bullshit. Here are some red flags to watch for:

1. Over-the-Top Promises

If someone claims they can double your revenue, guarantee results, or eliminate all your risks, run. There are no guarantees in business—anyone who tells you otherwise is lying.

2. Lack of Transparency

Legit professionals don't hide their terms, fees, or deliverables. If someone can't give you clear answers—or they dodge your questions—it's a sign they're not trustworthy.

3. High-Pressure Tactics

If someone's pushing you to "act now" or claiming the deal will disappear if you don't commit immediately, it's a bad sign. Real opportunities don't need to be rushed.

4. No Track Record

Always check credentials, reviews, and references. If someone can't prove they've delivered results for other clients, they have no business asking for your money.

5. Vague or Generic Advice

Scammers and hype artists rely on buzzwords and vague promises because they don't actually know what they're doing. If their pitch can't be backed up with specifics, walk away.

How to Protect Yourself

Avoiding scams isn't just about spotting red flags—it's about setting yourself up to make smarter decisions. Here's what's worked for me:

1. Do Your Homework

Before you commit to anything, research the hell out of it. Look up reviews, ask for references, and dig into the details. The more informed you are, the harder it is for someone to take advantage of you.

- Check the firm's license

- Ask for references

- Ask for the names of companies they have worked for

- Investigate their firm on the internet

- Ask your most trusted professional colleagues who run successful companies

2. Trust Your Gut

If something feels off, listen to that instinct. Your gut is often smarter than you realize.

3. Ask Questions

Don't be afraid to probe. How does this work? What do I get? What happens if it doesn't work out? Scammers hate questions—legit professionals welcome them.

4. Take Your Time

Scammers rely on urgency to pressure you into bad decisions. Slow down, think it through, and don't let anyone rush you.

5. Focus on the Fundamentals

Trends come and go, but the basics of running a business stay the same—serve your customers, manage your money, and deliver quality. If you focus on the fundamentals, you won't need to chase every shiny new thing.

The Bottom Line

Scams and hype are part of the business landscape. They prey on your ambition, your fear of missing out, and your desire to succeed. But if you keep your head on straight, you can avoid falling into the trap.

The key is to stay skeptical, do your homework, and never let desperation cloud your judgment. Remember—if something sounds too good to be true, it probably is.

Because in the world of business, the only real "guarantee" is that someone, somewhere, is going to try to sell you bullshit. Don't buy it.

"If it sounds too good to be true, it probably is." This is a widely used and effective saying to remind individuals to be cautious about unrealistic offers or opportunities, especially those promising quick riches.

Chapter 4: Employees— Who Are the "Keepers"?

Here's the hard truth: if you're trying to do everything yourself, you're not running a business—you're running yourself into the ground. I get it. Your company is your baby, and no one else can do things quite like you can. But here's the thing: you're not Superman, and even if you were, Superman doesn't do taxes, answer customer service emails, and manage five client projects at the same time. To take your business to the next level, you've got to learn to delegate.

Delegation isn't just about freeing up your time; it's about letting people who are *better* than you at certain things take the wheel. Yes, I said it. There are people out there who are better than you at specific tasks. That's not a knock on your abilities; it's just reality. You can't be a marketing genius, a financial wizard, a sales closer, and a tech guru all at once. And if you're trying to be, your business is going to stall out.

Characteristics of the "Keepers" to build your TEAM Finding the "Keepers"

1. Drive

I'm not talking about someone who just shows up to collect a paycheck. I want people who *give a damn.* People who are hungry to learn, eager to solve problems, and motivated to succeed—not just for themselves but for the team. Drive isn't something you can teach. Either someone has it, or they don't. And trust me, you'll know pretty quickly who's coasting and who's in it to win it.

2. Analytical Skills with Technology and AI

The world is changing fast, and if your employees can't keep up, your business won't either. I need people who are comfortable with data, know how to use AI tools, and can think critically about how technology impacts the bottom line. We're in an era where every industry—from construction to retail—is being reshaped by tech. If your team isn't tech-savvy, you're falling behind. Period.

3. Great Communication Skills

I don't care how smart someone is—if they can't communicate effectively, they're a liability. Whether it's explaining a complex idea, giving feedback, or just writing a clear email, communication is everything. It's the glue that holds your team together and the oil that keeps the machine running smoothly. I want people who can articulate their thoughts, listen actively, and collaborate without drama.

Retaining your "Keepers"

Now, let's talk about keeping these rock stars once you've found them. Because here's the deal: talent is expensive, and the best employees know their worth. If you're trying to build an elite team, you've got to treat them like one.

1. Pay More Than Market Value

Seriously, stop being cheap. If you want top-tier talent, you've got to pony up. I'm not talking about matching the industry average—I'm saying pay *at least* 20% more than the market rate. Money talks, and if you're not willing to pay for quality, someone else will.

2. Offer Perks That Matter

Forget the ping-pong tables and free snacks. Real perks are the ones that make people's lives better. Think health benefits, flexible schedules, professional development opportunities, and a warm, supportive office culture. Give your team the tools they need to do their job well—state-of-the-art computers, phones, software, whatever it takes. Make their work environment a place they actually *want* to be.

3. Give More Vacation

You know what burns people out? Working non-stop. You want your employees to be sharp, creative, and productive? Give them time to recharge. Offer at least a week more vacation than the standard. Trust me, they'll come back refreshed and ready to crush it.

4. Health Care & 401k

I always ask before hiring if the new employee needs these programs. I only offer health care to my employee only and the entire family would be additional lout of their pay or a nice bonus down the line.

5. Perks

Give them ½ days off once in a while, tickets to events, and allow them to attend holiday parties at the school of their children. Discuss the holidays they would like off during the year. I don't give them off every holiday, only the big ones like Christmas, Thanksgiving, July 4th, Memorial Day and Labor Day.

6. Company Handbook

You will be pleasantly surprised how much good employees appreciate a company handbook outlining all of your companies procedures and guidelines. The handbook will definitely protect you against the bad employees as everyone is required to read and sign off on the handbook each year.

Great employees are an investment, not an expense. Treat them well, and they'll help you take your business to heights you never thought possible. But if you try to cut corners, micromanage, or skimp on pay and perks, you'll be stuck in the same place—doing everything yourself and wondering why your business isn't growing.

But here's the good news: every bad employee is a chance to learn and grow as a leader. Over the years, I've developed some strategies for handling these situations, and while they're not always easy to implement, they've made a world of difference for me and my business.

If you're dealing with a bad employee right now (or worried you might in the future), let's talk about how to spot them, how to address the issues, and, if necessary, how to let them go.

The Types of Bad Employees I've Met

I've encountered a lot of different personalities over the years, but when it comes to "bad employees," there are a few types that stand out. Maybe you'll recognize some of these:

1. The Slacker

Oh, the Slacker. This is the person who does just enough to avoid getting fired. They're always on their phone, taking extra-long breaks, and disappearing when you need them most. They're not outright disruptive—they're just... not helpful.

2. The Know-It-All

Then there's the Know-It-All. This person loves to question your decisions, challenge your authority, and act like they know more about your business than you do. Every meeting with them feels like a debate, and you leave wondering why you even bothered.

3. The Drama Magnet

I've had my fair share of Drama Magnets. These are the employees who somehow manage to stir up conflict wherever they go. They're always gossiping, always complaining, and always dragging everyone else into their mess.

4. The Over-Promiser, Under-Deliverer

This one might be the most frustrating of all. They come in with big promises during the interview, making you think you've struck gold. But once they're on the job, they can't seem to follow through on anything.

5. The Toxic Saboteur

And then there's the Toxic Saboteur. Thankfully, I've only had to deal with this type a couple of times, but once is enough. This is the person who actively undermines you, spreads negativity, and might even try to sabotage the business. They're not just bad at their job—they're dangerous.

The Wake-Up Call

I'll be honest with you: the first few times I dealt with a bad employee, I ignored the problem. I told myself things like, *They're just having a rough patch,* or *Maybe it's something I'm doing wrong.* But here's what I've learned: ignoring the problem doesn't make it go away. In fact, it usually makes it worse.

The longer you let a bad employee stick around, the more damage they can do—to your business, to your team, and to your own sense of confidence as a leader.

Setting the expectations for Employees in everyday work hours

1. Get to the Root of the Problem by talking to them and asking them questions

The first step is figuring out what's really going on. Is this person truly a bad employee, or are they just in the wrong role? Are they struggling with personal issues, or do they need more training?

I've found that sitting down for an honest conversation can reveal a lot. Sometimes, the problem is fixable. Other times, it's not. But you won't know until you ask.

2. Set Clear Expectations

Early on, I made the mistake of assuming people just "knew" what was expected of them. Spoiler alert: they don't.

Now, I make it a point to set clear, measurable expectations for every employee. I put it in writing, whether it's a detailed job description, a performance plan, or even just an email. That way, there's no confusion about what I need from them.

3. Offer Feedback and Support

If an employee is struggling, I try to help them before jumping to conclusions. Maybe they need additional training, a mentor, or even just a little encouragement.

That said, feedback only works if the employee is willing to listen and make an effort. If they're defensive, dismissive, or unwilling to change, then we've got a bigger problem.

4. Know When to Let Go

This is the hardest part, especially if you're a small business owner who feels personally connected to your team. But sometimes, the best thing you can do—for yourself, for your business, and even for the employee—is to let them go.

I've had to fire people before, and it's never fun. But every time I've done it, I've felt an enormous sense of relief afterward. Because the truth is, keeping a bad employee around out of guilt or fear will only hurt your business in the long run.

5. Hold Weekly Staff Meetings

This keeps everyone on the same page and allows your assistant to take notes and record all topics covered. This may help save you when you fire an employee and claim certain company policies were never discussed.

I pulled her aside, explained how her behavior was affecting the team, and gave her a chance to improve. When she didn't, I let her go. Almost immediately, the office felt lighter, and morale improved.

Building a Stronger Team

The current generations of employees want to feel they have a perspective heard on running and building the company. Therefore, I encourage them to take
ownership" For every bad employee, there are plenty of great ones out there. By focusing on building a strong, motivated team, you'll create a business that runs smoothly—and a work environment you're proud of.

"Treat employees like they make a difference, and they will." – **Jim Goodnight, CEO of SAS Institute**

Chapter 5: Business Partner Pros and Cons

Deciding whether you need or want a business partner is a big deal, it's like getting married, but with spreadsheets and tax forms. Here's how to figure out if bringing someone into your business is the right move for you.

Ask Yourself: Why Do I Want a Partner?

Before you start shopping for someone to share the load, get brutally honest with yourself. What's your motivation? Here are some common reasons people look for a partner:

- **You Need Complementary Skills**: Maybe you're a marketing wizard, but spreadsheets make your eyes glaze over. A partner with complementary strengths can fill those gaps.

- **You Need Additional Resources**: Whether it's financial backing, industry connections, or access to a particular market, a partner can bring assets you don't have.

- **You Want Shared Responsibility**: Running a business can be lonely and overwhelming. A partner can share the workload, decision-making, and risk.

- **You Crave Accountability**: If you are a person who struggles with procrastination or staying focused on long-term goals, a partner can help keep you on track.

If your reason is, "I'm scared to go it alone," pause and think. Fear is natural, but it's not the best reason to bring someone into your business.

2. Consider the Pros of Having a Partner

- **Shared Workload**: Let's face it—there are only so many hours in a day. A good partner can help lighten the load.

- **Diverse Perspectives**: Two heads are (sometimes) better than one. A partner might bring fresh ideas and challenge your thinking.

- **Shared Risk**: It's nice to know you're not carrying all the risk on your own shoulders.

- **Bigger Network**: A partner might bring connections you'd never have access to on your own.

---

3. Weigh the Cons of Having a Partner

- **Loss of Control**: You're no longer the sole decision-maker. Every major choice now requires agreement.

- **Profit Sharing**: You're splitting the pie, which means less money in your pocket.

- **Potential Conflict**: Disagreements are inevitable, and if they're not handled well, they can sink the business—or the relationship.

- **Uneven Contribution**: What happens if you feel like you're doing all the work while your partner coasts? Resentment can build fast.

---

4. Do You Have the Right Personality for a Partnership?

Not everyone is cut out to work with a partner. Ask yourself:

- Are you comfortable sharing control and decision-making?

- Can you handle disagreements without taking them personally?

- Are you willing to compromise?

- Do you trust others enough to delegate critical tasks?

If the thought of someone else having a say in *your* business makes your blood boil, a partnership might not be for you.

---

5. What to Look for in a Partner

If you've decided you're open to a partner, finding the *right* one is crucial. Here's what to look for:

- **Complementary Skills**: A partner should bring strengths that you lack. If you're great at sales but terrible at operations, find someone who thrives in that area.

- **Shared Vision**: You need to agree on where the business is headed and what success looks like.

- **Aligned Values**: If your partner has a wildly different work ethic or ethical compass, it's a recipe for disaster.

- **Trust**: If you wouldn't trust them with your bank account, don't trust them with your business.

- **Commitment**: Make sure they're as invested in the business as you are.

---

6. Alternatives to a Full Partnership

Not sure you're ready to go all-in with a partner? There are other ways to get the help you need without giving up equity:

- **Hire Specialized Help**: Bring on freelancers, contractors, or employees to fill skill gaps.

- **Consultants or Advisors**: Pay for expert advice without giving up control.

- **Equity Stakeholders**: Offer a small percentage of equity in exchange for specific contributions like funding or expertise, without making them a full partner.

7. The Bottom Line

A partnership can be the best decision you ever make—or the biggest headache of your life. The key is knowing yourself, your business, and what you truly need. If you're crystal clear on your goals, pick the right person, and set clear expectations from day one, a partner can help you scale faster, work smarter, and achieve more. But if you rush into it or pick the wrong person? You might be better off flying solo.

Take your time. This isn't just a business decision, it's a relationship. Choose wisely.

You know what's worse than dealing with a difficult client or a lawsuit? Dealing with a bad business partner. Because here's the kicker: you're stuck with them. A bad partner is like being married to someone who doesn't just snore but also sets the house on fire while you sleep. At first, everything seemed great. You had big plans, shared dreams, and maybe even a few celebratory beers after signing the paperwork. But now? Now you're wondering if they're the worst decision you've ever made.

There are a few flavors of bad business partners, and they all suck in their own special way.

1. The Ghost

This is the partner who disappears the moment real work shows up. They were full of ideas and energy in the beginning, but now? Crickets. You're pulling all-nighters, juggling a thousand tasks, and they're...posting vacation photos on Instagram.

The Ghost loves to talk about *our* company but seems to think *you're* the one who should actually run it. They show up for the big moments—the pitch meetings, the awards, the glory—but when it's time to grind, they vanish. If you're doing 90% of the work while they "supervise," congratulations, you've found yourself a Ghost.

2. The Thief

This one's a gut punch. The Thief is the partner who, at some point, decides that what's yours is also theirs—your money, your clients, your ideas. Maybe they're skimming off the top. Maybe they're stealing credit for your hard work. Maybe they've even got a secret side hustle that's competing with your business.

Here's the thing about The Thief: they don't just steal stuff; they steal trust. And once trust is gone, your partnership is toast. You can't build a business with someone who's more focused on lining their own pockets than building something together.

3. The "Like-Vision" Dreamer

This one's tricky because they're not toxic—they're just...useless. The Like-Vision partner loves to dream big, just like you. They're all about brainstorming, vision boards, and inspirational quotes. But when it comes to execution? Forget it.

They'll talk for hours about what the company *could* be while ignoring what it actually *needs* to be right now. You're trying to solve today's problems, and they're busy planning a product launch that's five years away. It's like trying to build a house with someone who won't stop talking about where the pool should go.

4. The Opposite Goals Saboteur

This is the partner who doesn't just have different goals—they have *opposite* goals. You want to grow the business; they want to keep it small and manageable. You want to reinvest profits; they want to pull every dime out for themselves. You're aiming for the moon, and they're happy lounging in the backyard.

The Saboteur isn't necessarily doing it on purpose—they might genuinely believe their way is better. But the result is the same: constant conflict, stalled progress, and a partnership that feels more like a tug-of-war than a team effort.

How to Handle It

So, what do you do when your business partner turns out to be a dud? Here's the no-BS answer: it depends on how bad it is.

1. Have the Hard Conversation

First, you've got to confront the issue head-on. I know, it's awkward. No one likes conflict. But if you're tiptoeing around the problem, it's only going to get worse. Sit down, lay out the facts, and be brutally honest. "Hey, I feel like I'm doing all the heavy lifting," or "I'm concerned about where the money's going," or "We don't seem to be on the same page about the future of this business."

If they're reasonable, this conversation might actually fix things. If they're not, well...that's a different story.

2. Check the Paperwork

Remember that partnership agreement you (hopefully) signed when you started the business? Now's the time to dig it out and see what your options are. A good agreement should outline what happens if one partner wants out, if there's a dispute, or if someone's not pulling their weight. If you don't have an agreement? You're in for a rough ride.

3. Protect Yourself

If the situation involves theft or shady behavior, you've got to take action—fast. Lock down the finances, change the passwords, and talk to a lawyer before things spiral out of control. The last thing you want is for their bad decisions to sink the whole ship.

4. Cut the Cord

Sometimes, the only solution is to end the partnership. This isn't easy, especially if you're emotionally invested or if they're a close friend or family member. But at the end of the day, your business can't thrive with dead weight dragging it down.

And let me say this loud and clear: it's better to go it alone than to stay stuck with a bad partner. Yes, it's scary. Yes, it's going to be messy. But staying in a toxic partnership will cost you more in the long run—money, time, and your sanity.

The Lesson

A great business partner can take your company to heights you never imagined. A bad one can destroy everything you've built. The key is to choose wisely, pay attention to red flags, and never be afraid to walk away if it's not working.

Because here's the truth: your business is too important to let someone else screw it up. You worked too hard to get here. Don't let a bad partner hold you back.

"Emphasize the need for clear communication, aligned visions, and a healthy dose of caution when bringing someone on board." - **Tony Robbins**

Chapter 6: Government - Dancing with the Bureaucratic Devil

Ah, the government. The one business partner you didn't choose but are stuck with anyway. They don't contribute to your bottom line, they don't help you grow, and yet they're always there— watching, regulating, and demanding their cut. Dealing with government red tape is like trying to run a marathon with your shoelaces tied together. Annoying? Yes. Avoidable? Absolutely not.

If you're an entrepreneur, you've already figured out that the government doesn't make anything easy. Whether it's permits, taxes, inspections, or compliance, every step feels like an obstacle course designed by someone who hates small business owners. And the people enforcing these regulations? Well, let's just say they're not exactly known for their hustle or customer service skills.

The Maze of Government Red Tape

You've got big plans, but before you can break ground, sell your product, or even open your doors, you've got to deal with a mountain of paperwork. Licenses, permits, certifications—it's like they want to see how much patience you have before they let you do anything.

Here's the kicker: it's never just one form. No, sir. It's form A, which requires form B, but you can't get form B until you've filed form C. And by the time you've completed everything, the rules have probably changed, and you've got to start over.

The worst part? Half the time, even the people working for the government don't seem to know what's going on. You'll call one office, and they'll give you one answer. Then you'll call another, and they'll tell you the exact opposite. It's like some kind of cruel game where the rules are made up on the spot.

Dealing with Government Employees

Let's get one thing straight: not all government employees are terrible. Some are genuinely helpful. But a lot? A lot seem to be allergic to effort. You'll walk into an office, and the vibe is less "How can I help you?" and more "Why are you bothering me?" They're shuffling papers, taking long coffee breaks, and acting like your questions about starting or running your business are a personal inconvenience.

The key here is patience, persistence, and, honestly, a little bit of charm. Be polite, but don't let them brush you off. If you're not getting the answers you need, escalate. Ask for a supervisor. Call back. Show up in person if you have to. You're not trying to make friends—you're trying to get your business moving.

Regulations: The Necessary Evil

Look, I'm not going to pretend that all regulations are bad. Some of them exist for a reason. You probably don't want your competitors selling toxic products or building unsafe structures, right? But let's be real—there's a difference between reasonable regulations and the bureaucratic overreach that makes you want to slam your head against your desk.

The trick is to understand the rules that actually matter and ignore the noise. Yes, you have to follow the laws, but don't let yourself get bogged down by every little detail. Hire a good accountant, find a lawyer who knows your industry, and let them help you navigate the madness.

Surviving the Tax Man

Let's not forget everyone's least favorite part of running a business: taxes. The government doesn't care if you're struggling, if you're reinvesting in your company, or if you just had a bad quarter. They want their money, and they want it on time.

Here's my advice: Pay yourself a regular paycheck like the employees. Don't cut corners, don't play games, and for the love of God, don't try to cheat the system. The IRS doesn't mess around, and getting on their bad side is a surefire way to tank your business. But also don't overpay. Work with a tax professional who knows how to find every deduction and credit you're entitled to. The goal is to pay what you owe—nothing more, nothing less.

The Most Frustrating Regulations I've Faced

Over the years, I've run into some truly head-scratching regulations. Here are a few that still make me shake my head:

1. The Permit Maze

One time, I needed a simple permit to open a new location for my business. What I thought would be a one-step process turned into a nightmare of applications, inspections, and approvals. At one point, I had to get a permit for the permit I was applying for. I wish I were joking.

2. The Tax Filing Circus

Taxes are a whole other beast. Between federal, state, and local taxes, there's always something to file, some form to fill out, or some deadline to meet. One year, I accidentally filled out the wrong form, and it took me *months* to untangle the mess.

3. The "Invisible" Rules

Then there are the regulations you don't even know exist until you're in trouble. Like the time I found out I needed a special license to sell a product in a certain state. No one told me until after

I'd already started selling—and let's just say the fines weren't cheap.

How I've Learned to Handle It

If dealing with government red tape is unavoidable, the key is learning how to manage it without losing your mind. Here's what's worked for me:

1. Get Comfortable Asking Questions

One of the biggest mistakes I made early on was assuming I had to figure everything out on my own. Now, I'm not afraid to ask questions—lots of them. Whether it's calling a government office, consulting with a lawyer, or even asking fellow business owners for advice, I've learned that there's no shame in admitting you don't know something.

2. Stay Organized

Red tape thrives in chaos. If you're not organized, it's easy to miss deadlines, lose important documents, or forget which forms you've already filled out. I keep a dedicated folder (both physical and digital) for all my business-related paperwork, and I use a calendar to track every deadline. It's not glamorous, but it works.

3. Hire Help When You Need It

Let me be real with you: sometimes, it's worth paying someone else to deal with the headaches. Whether it's an accountant to handle your taxes or a lawyer to review contracts, having an expert in your corner can save you time, money, and a whole lot of stress.

4. Break It Down

When you're staring at a huge, complicated process, it's easy to feel overwhelmed. I've learned to break things down into smaller, manageable steps. Instead of focusing on the entire process, I focus on the next thing I need to do. One step at a time, and before you know it, you're done.

Getting Audited can feel like a gut punch, but it doesn't have to derail your business if you handle it right. First, stay calm—most audits aren't a witch hunt; they're just a detailed review. Gather all requested documents promptly, stay organized, and be transparent. If you've been keeping clean, detailed financial records (and you should be!), this will make the process much smoother. Don't try to wing it—get professional help from your bookkeeper, accountant or tax attorney to ensure everything is in order and to handle any tricky questions BEFORE the AUDIT. Most importantly, treat the auditor with respect and professionalism; being combative or evasive will only make things worse. An audit is stressful, but if you've been running your business by the book, it's more of an inconvenience than a disaster.

Lessons Learned

If there's one thing I've learned about government red tape, it's this: it's not going away, so you might as well learn how to deal with it. Stay organized, ask for help when you need it, and don't be afraid to laugh at the absurdity of it all. At the end of the day, it's just another part of running a business. And while it's not fun, it's a challenge you can absolutely overcome.

Next up, we're diving into something a little more exciting: marketing missteps and the lessons I've learned from failed campaigns. Trust me, you won't want to miss this one. Stay tuned.

"We've got great potential in our country and the only way we're going to make sure kids are getting the degrees that they need, make sure we're getting through that red tape, is by working together." - **Amy Klobuchar**

Chapter 7: Marketing Art of a Great Company Plan

Let's talk about marketing. It's the lifeblood of your business, the thing that keeps customers coming through the door

When I first started my entrepreneurial journey, I believed that a great marketing plan was the key to success. You know the drill: polished presentations, bulletproof spreadsheets, and a narrative so compelling it could bring investors to tears. But what I didn't realize was that marketing a company plan—whether to investors, employees, or customers—is a whole art form steeped in bullshit. And here's the kicker: everyone does it, no matter how authentic they claim to be.

Welcome to the world of spinning reality into a story that sells. This chapter isn't just about identifying the bullshit; it's about learning how to package it, navigate it, and, yes, survive it. Because trust me, no matter how great your company plan is, you'll run into bullshit that derails your vision. It's inevitable.

The Bullshit of the "Perfect Plan"

Every CEO or entrepreneur will eventually craft what they believe is a genius company plan. It's got everything: market analysis, revenue projections, competitive advantages, and a roadmap to world domination. You'll spend hours obsessing over the font choice in your pitch deck, thinking it somehow conveys trustworthiness or innovation. (Spoiler: It doesn't. No one cares about your font.)

But here's the truth no one tells you: **your plan is just a story**. And like every story, it's full of holes. Investors know this. Customers know this. Hell, even you know this if you're being honest. But you'll still be expected to present it as if it's infallible. Why? Because people want to believe in the illusion of certainty.

The first time I pitched a company plan to investors, I thought I was prepared. I had charts, graphs, and a narrative arc that would make a Hollywood screenwriter jealous. But then came the questions:

- "What happens if your primary market dries up?"

- "What's your contingency for a competitor undercutting your prices?"

- "How are you planning to scale without burning through cash?"

I had answers, of course—but they were mostly educated guesses wrapped in confident delivery. And that's the game: *it's not about having the perfect plan; it's about making people believe you do.*

The Art of Selling the Dream

Marketing a company plan is not about the data; it's about the dream. People—whether they're investors, employees, or customers—don't buy into companies; they buy into stories. Your job is to craft a narrative that makes them feel like they're part of something bigger.

But here's the problem: dreams are subjective. What excites one person might bore another. That's why you have to tailor your bullshit to your audience. Let me break it down:

1. **To Investors:** They want returns. Your story needs to scream, "This is a money printer." Talk about scale, market dominance, and exit strategies. Sprinkle in some industry buzzwords like "disruption," "synergy," or my personal

favorite, "proprietary technology." It doesn't matter if your tech is just a slightly better mousetrap—call it proprietary, and suddenly it's worth millions.

2. **To Employees**: They want purpose. Sell them on the mission, the culture, and the chance to be part of something groundbreaking. This is where you talk about "changing the world" or "redefining industries." Never mind that 90% of startups fail; the goal is to make them believe they're part of the 10%.

3. **To Customers**: They want solutions. Your bullshit here needs to be practical, not aspirational. Talk about how your product or service will solve their pain points, even if you're oversimplifying the problem. Overpromise, but under-deliver just enough that they'll stick around for version 2.0.

Navigating the Unexpected Bullshit

Of course, no matter how well you market your plan, bullshit will find its way in. Here are a few examples of the unexpected nonsense you'll encounter—and how to deal with it:

1. **The "Pivot Parade":**

   At some point, someone will suggest pivoting your business model. Maybe your investors get cold feet, or the market shifts, or a competitor beats you to the punch. Suddenly, your perfect plan is obsolete. The key here is to embrace the pivot without panicking. Remember, **a pivot isn't failure; it's adaptation.** Just make sure to spin it as a strategic move, not a desperate one.

2. **The "Copycat Curse":**

You'll come up with what you think is a revolutionary idea, only to discover that three other companies are already doing it—and they're better funded. This is where your marketing skills come into play. Differentiate yourself, even if it's just cosmetic. Sometimes, the perception of innovation is more important than the reality of it.

3. **The "Team Turmoil":**

Nothing derails a great company plan faster than internal conflict. Whether it's a co-founder disagreement or a toxic employee, you'll have to manage egos and emotions while keeping the ship steady. My advice? **Be ruthless when necessary.** A great plan won't survive a dysfunctional team.

Lessons in the Art of Bullshit

If I've learned anything from marketing company plans, it's this: *bullshit is a skill, not a flaw.* The goal isn't to deceive; it's to inspire, persuade, and adapt. Here are a few final tips:

- *Confidence is king.* People will believe your plan if you believe it yourself. Even if you're unsure, act like you're not.

- *Simplify the complex.* No one wants to wade through a 50-page business plan. Boil it down to the essentials and make it digestible.

- *Be ready to pivot.* The best plans are flexible. Always have a backup narrative for when things go sideways.

Marketing a company plan is an art, not a science. It's about balancing ambition with pragmatism, truth with storytelling, and vision with execution. And yes, it's about navigating bullshit with a smile on your face and a plan in your back pocket.

And—if we're being honest—one of the easiest ways to flush money down the toilet if you're not careful. Every entrepreneur has launched a marketing campaign that flopped harder than a bad first date. I'm no exception. But the beauty of failure? It's a hell of a teacher.

So, let's break down some of the biggest marketing mistakes I've made (and seen others make) and the lessons they taught me.

---

1. Know Your Target Audience

Here's how most bad marketing campaigns start: you assume you know who your audience is, but you don't. You think your product is perfect for *everyone*, so you try to sell it to *everyone*. Spoiler alert: it doesn't work.

Let me tell you about one of my first big missteps. I spent thousands on an ad campaign targeting a broad demographic—basically anyone who had a pulse. The result? Crickets. Why? Because I hadn't done my homework. I didn't know who actually *needed* my product, who would *pay* for it, or how to *speak their language*.

Lesson learned: You've got to narrow it down. *Who are your customers and who needs my product?* What are their problems? How do they spend their money? The clearer your picture of your audience, the more effective your marketing will be.

2. Know Your Territory

Here's another classic screw-up: trying to sell in a market that doesn't want what you're offering. You could have the best product in the world, but if you're pitching it to the wrong crowd, it's game over.

Case in point: I once tried to launch a premium product in a price-sensitive market. I thought I could "educate" people on why my product was worth the higher price. Turns out, they weren't interested in education—they just wanted the cheapest option available. That campaign didn't just fail; it belly-flopped.

The takeaway? Know your territory. Research your market. Understand the local culture, the competition, and the demand. Don't try to force something that doesn't fit.

---

3. Know What You Produce Best

Here's a harsh reality: you're not going to be good at everything. You might think you can branch out into new products, new services, new whatever—but if it's not in your wheelhouse, you're setting yourself up for failure.

Stick the aspect of your business that comes the easiest and you make the most money—and then become the best/elite in that area. Focus on the products or services you can produce with the least amount of effort while maintaining the highest quality. That's where your profit margin lives.

4. Focus Ahead with Your Entire Team

Here's a mistake that happens way too often: the marketing team is running one way, the sales team is running another, and operations is sitting there wondering what the hell is going on. If your team isn't aligned, your marketing will fail. Period.

I've been guilty of this. I'd launch a marketing campaign without looping in the rest of the team. The result? Sales didn't know how to close the leads, customer service wasn't prepared to handle the influx, and production couldn't keep up with demand. It was chaos.

The fix? Get everyone on the same page. Before you launch a campaign, make sure your entire team understands the goal, the strategy, and their role in making it a success. Marketing isn't a solo act—it's a team sport.

---

5. Lessons Learned from Failed Campaigns

Fail Fast, Fail Cheap

Not every campaign is going to be a home run, and that's okay. The key is to test small, learn quickly, and pivot if necessary. Don't blow your entire budget on an unproven idea. Start small, measure the results, and scale up if it works.

Track Everything-Have weekly marketing meetings to discuss processes and then monthly meetings to discuss the numbers— where are the numbers working. Where are the sales coming from. If you wait until the end of the year to look at the statistics, you could be spending tens of thousands on a failed platform.

If you're not tracking your marketing efforts, you're flying blind. Use analytics, customer feedback, and sales data to figure out what's working and what's not. Numbers don't lie.

Be Willing to Adapt

One of the biggest mistakes you can make is falling in love with your own ideas. Just because you think a campaign is brilliant doesn't mean your audience will. If something isn't working, don't dig in your heels—adapt.

Simpler is Better

Sometimes, we overcomplicate things. We try to be clever, flashy, or groundbreaking, and the message gets lost. The best campaigns are often the simplest ones. Focus on solving a problem, communicating value, and making it easy for customers to say yes.

The Power of Focus

At the end of the day, successful marketing isn't about doing everything, it's about doing the *right* things. Know your audience. Know your market. Play to your strengths. And most importantly, focus. Don't scatter your resources across a million different ideas. Pick a direction, commit to it, and bring your entire team along for the ride.

Marketing is a game of strategy, not luck. When you approach it with focus and discipline, you'll stop making costly mistakes and start seeing real results. And when you fail—and trust me, you will—learn from it, adjust, and come back stronger. That's how you win.

"While marketing errors can impact brand perception, reality and consistent effort can correct this over time." - **Elon Musk**

Chapter 8: Broke, Desperate, and Begging the Bank

Let me set the scene: you're sitting in a bank lobby, sweating through your shirt. Your stomach is in knots, not because you had a bad breakfast, but because you're broke. Not just "tight on cash" broke—I mean broke-broke. Payroll is due in five days, your vendors are calling nonstop, and your personal credit cards are maxed out. All you've got left is hope, and even that's running on fumes.

If you haven't been there yet, let me assure you: it's coming. Every CEO or entrepreneur eventually faces this moment. Maybe it's the result of a bad decision, a market downturn, or just plain bad luck. Whatever the cause, you're now in the one position no one talks about in the glossy business magazines: desperate, broke, and begging the bank.

This chapter isn't about how to avoid this situation—because, let's be honest, sometimes it's unavoidable. Instead, I'm going to walk you through how to survive it, how to keep your dignity intact (or as intact as possible), and how to turn desperation into an opportunity. Yes, there's bullshit involved—tons of it—but that's the game. Let's play.

The Anatomy of Desperation

First, let's get one thing straight: banks don't care about your desperation. In fact, they can smell it on you the moment you walk in the door. The loan officer you're about to meet? They've seen a hundred versions of you this month alone. You're not special.

Here's what I've learned: desperation is a liability. The more desperate you seem, the less likely you are to get what you want. Banks don't lend to people who need money; they lend to people who seem like they don't. It's a paradox, but it's the truth.

So, before you step foot into that bank, you need to do one thing: get your act together. I don't care if you're on the verge of a breakdown—fake it. Walk in there like you've got options, even if your only other option is selling your car to make payroll.

The Bullshit You'll Face

Let me prepare you for what's coming. Banks have a way of making you feel like they're doing you a favor, even though they'll profit handsomely from your misery. Here are some classics you'll encounter:

1. **The "Risk Assessment" Speech:**

   "Your business doesn't meet our lending criteria at this time." Translation? You're too risky, and they don't want to deal with you unless you've got something to offer as collateral—preferably your firstborn child.

2. **The "We Believe in You" Lie:**

   "We see potential in your business, and we'd love to help, but..." That "but" is where they'll hit you with a ridiculous interest rate, a request for personal guarantees, or loan terms so restrictive you'll feel like you're signing away your soul.

3. **The "Paperwork Pile-Up":**

"We just need a few more documents." This is their way of stalling while they figure out if you're worth the trouble. Get ready to provide everything from last year's tax returns to the blood type of your CFO.

How to Play the Game

I've been in that chair, staring across the desk at a loan officer who could make or break my business with a single decision. Here's what I've learned about how to play the game:

1. **Control the Narrative:**

Don't let them see you sweat. Frame your situation as a temporary cash-flow issue, not a full-on collapse. Use phrases like "We're experiencing rapid growth, and we need additional capital to scale" instead of "We're drowning, and I'm two weeks away from selling my kidney."

2. **Bring Receipts (Literally):**

Banks love to see data. Show them your financials, your projections, and your plan for paying them back. The more prepared you are, the harder it is for them to say no. Even if your numbers are ugly, present them with confidence.

3. **Negotiate Like You Have Options:**

Even if the bank is your last resort, act like you've got other lenders lined up. Say things like, "I'm exploring a few financing options, but I wanted to give you the first look." It's pure bullshit, but it works.

4. **Collateral is King:**

If you're broke, you probably don't have much to offer as collateral but get creative. Equipment, inventory, even personal assets can be leveraged. Just be careful—you don't want to lose your house over a bad deal.

5. **Build Relationships Before You Need Them:**

This one's a long game, but it's crucial. If you wait until you're desperate to build a relationship with your banker, you've already lost. Start fostering those relationships early, even when you don't need money. That way, when you do, they'll be more inclined to help.

The Emotional Toll

Let's talk about the emotional side of this, because no one else will. Begging the bank isn't just humiliating—it's soul-crushing. You'll feel like a failure, like you've let everyone down. And the worst part? You'll start to believe your own bullshit: "Maybe I'm not cut out for this. Maybe this really is the end."

Here's what I want you to remember: this moment doesn't define you. Every successful entrepreneur has been here. Steve Jobs? Fired from his own company. Elon Musk? Slept on friends' couches while trying to get Tesla off the ground. The difference between those who make it and those who don't isn't the absence of failure—it's the ability to keep going.

Turning Desperation into Opportunity

Believe it or not, there's a silver lining to being broke and desperate: it forces you to get creative. When your back is against the wall, you'll find solutions you never would have considered otherwise. Maybe it's a strategic partnership, a renegotiation with vendors, or a new revenue stream you hadn't explored. Desperation can either crush you or push you to innovate. Choose the latter.

The Takeaway

If you're reading this and you're in the middle of your own "broke and begging" moment, let me leave you with this:

1. You're not alone. Every entrepreneur faces this at some point. It's part of the journey.

2. Desperation is temporary. Your current situation doesn't define your future.

3. Bullshit is a skill. Learn to sell your story, even when the odds are against you.

And finally, remember this: the bank isn't doing you a favor. You're giving them an opportunity to make money off your success. Walk in there like you believe that, even if you don't. Fake it till you make it, because sometimes that's the only way to survive.

This chapter of your life may be messy, humiliating, and downright terrifying—but it's also where resilience is born. And that, my friend, is priceless.

in a rough spot—y' know, the exact moment you actually need help—they'll make you jump through flaming hoops just for the chance to be rejected.

Step One: Get Your Financial House in Order

If you're going to ask a bank for money, you'd better have your financials looking sharp. No excuses, no half-assed spreadsheets, and definitely no "I think I left that document somewhere" nonsense.

1. Hire a Bookkeeper and CPA

I don't care if you're great with numbers—hire professionals. A good bookkeeper keeps your records clean and organized, while a CPA makes sure your taxes and financial strategies are on point. These people are like your financial bodyguards, and you'll need them when the bank starts asking questions.

2. Have Your Profit and Loss Statement Ready

The first thing a bank wants to see is your profit and loss statement. If you don't have one—or if it looks like it was thrown together during a lunch break—don't even bother showing up. Your P&L needs to be clear, accurate, and professional.

3. Know Your Numbers

This one's crucial. Don't just hand over your financials—understand them. If the loan officer asks about your cash flow, profit margins, or debt-to-income ratio, you'd better have answers. Nothing kills your chances faster than looking clueless.

Step Two: Brace Yourself for Extra Scrutiny

Being self-employed is great—until you need a loan. Then it's like you're wearing a giant neon sign that says "High Risk." Banks are going to grill you about everything: your income, your expenses, your business plan, your ability to repay. And you'd better have good answers.

1. Show Stability

Banks love stability. They want to see that your business has been around for a while, that your income is consistent, and that you're not just winging it. If you've got long-term clients, contracts, or recurring revenue, show them.

2. Collateral is King

Here's the harsh truth: banks don't care about your dreams; they care about getting their money back. If you're asking for a loan, they'll want collateral—something they can seize if you don't pay up. This could be equipment, property, or even personal assets.

3. Be Ready to Explain

Why do you need the money? How will you use it? How are you going to pay it back? You need to have clear, detailed answers to these questions. If you walk in without a plan, you're wasting everyone's time.

Step Three: Know Exactly What You Need

One of the biggest mistakes entrepreneurs make is asking for the wrong amount. Ask for too little, and the bank thinks you haven't planned well. Ask for too much, and they think you're reckless.

Calculate the Right Amount

Figure out how much you need to get through your cash crunch—then add a little buffer. Things rarely go as planned, and you don't want to end up back in the red a few months later.

Be Realistic About Repayment

Don't ask for a loan you can't afford to pay back. Banks aren't in the business of taking risks, so make sure your repayment plan is rock-solid.

Step Four: If the Bank Says No, Don't Panic

If the bank shuts you down, it's not the end of the world. There are other ways to get financing.

1. Lines of Credit

A line of credit is like a financial safety net. You only borrow what you need, and you only pay interest on what you use.

2. SBA Loans

The Small Business Administration backs loans specifically for small business owners. The process is slow and tedious, but the terms can be worth it.

3. Hard Money Lenders

Borrowing from a hard money lender can be a lifeline for entrepreneurs who need quick access to capital, especially when traditional banks won't lend. The pros include faster approval times, less emphasis on credit scores, and the ability to leverage assets like real estate as collateral. However, the cons are significant: hard money loans often come with sky-high interest rates, short repayment terms, and the risk of losing your collateral if you default. While they can be useful in emergencies, hard money loans should be a last resort due to their cost and potential financial strain. I will consider this if I have a considerable amount of sales materializing in 9-18 months and I feel very confident these sales will not default so I can pay back the hard money loan.

The Bullshit You Have to Deal With

Running out of money isn't fun, but it's not the end. It's part of the business bullshit we all deal with. The key is to stay calm, get your financials in order, and walk into that bank with confidence. Banks may not make it easy, but if you believe in your business—and show them why they should, too—you've got a fighting chance.

*"We never got tons of money to start Nando's ... it was done trench by trench, we had to duck and dive." - **Robert Brozin (Nandos)***

Chapter 9: Hiring the Right Team for the Company

Hiring the right team is one of the most critical tasks for any CEO or entrepreneur. A great team will elevate your business and make you look like a genius. A bad team, on the other hand, will drain your energy, blow your budget, and sabotage your vision before it even gets off the ground. And here's the kicker: you won't always know which one you've hired until it's too late.

This chapter isn't about writing job descriptions or conducting interviews. It's about the messy, unpredictable reality of hiring—and how to deal with the bullshit that comes with it.

The Illusion of the "Perfect" Candidate

Let me tell you about the first time I hired someone. I had a very specific idea of what I was looking for: someone smart, experienced, and passionate about the company's mission. I spent weeks obsessing over resumes, looking for that magical unicorn who checked every box. When I finally found someone who seemed perfect on paper, I hired them on the spot.

Big mistake.

Within three months, it became clear that this "perfect" candidate wasn't so perfect after all. They were great at talking the talk but couldn't deliver when it mattered. That's when I learned a harsh lesson: the perfect candidate doesn't exist.

Resumes lie. Interviews are performances. And references? Half the time, they're just friends who've agreed to say nice things. The truth is, hiring isn't about finding someone flawless—it's about finding someone who's the right fit for your team and your business, imperfections and all.

The Bullshit You'll Face When Hiring

Hiring is supposed to be straightforward: you need help, you find someone qualified, and they join your team. But in reality, it's a circus, and you're the ringmaster. Here's some of the bullshit you'll inevitably encounter:

1. **The Overconfident Candidate:**

   These people will sell themselves like they're God's gift to your industry. They'll use every buzzword in the book— "team player," "problem solver," "self-starter"—and make you believe they can single-handedly save your company. But nine times out of ten, they're all talk and no action.

2. **The Disappearing Act:**

   Ever had someone ace the interview, accept the offer, and then vanish without a trace? Welcome to the world of ghosting, where candidates disappear faster than your marketing budget.

3. **The Resume Exaggerator:**

   "Proficient in six coding languages"? Turns out they barely know one. "Led a team of 50"? More like interned in an office of 50. People will exaggerate their skills and experience to get the job, and it's up to you to separate fact from fiction.

4. **The Cultural Fit Conundrum:**

   Everyone talks about "hiring for culture," but no one tells you how subjective that is. What one person sees as a "collaborative spirit," another sees as "annoyingly chatty."

Culture fit is important, but it's also one of the biggest sources of hiring headaches.

Building a Team That Lasts

The ultimate goal is to build a team that not only helps your business succeed but also makes your life easier. When you've got the right people in the right roles, everything just clicks. But getting to that point takes time, patience, and a willingness to wade through the bullshit.

Here's what I've learned about building a lasting team:

1. **Invest in Your People:**

   Training, mentorship, and opportunities for growth are the best ways to keep your team engaged and motivated. People want to feel like they're part of something bigger than they are.

2. **Define Your Culture:**

   Be clear about what your company stands for and what kind of people thrive in your environment. This will make it easier to identify the right candidates—and weed out the wrong ones.

3. **Communicate, Communicate, Communicate:**

   Most workplace issues stem from poor communication. Make sure your team knows your expectations, goals, and vision. The more aligned everyone is, the better they'll perform.

4. **Keep Your Eyes Open:**

   If you have a great team member, always continue to evaluate as they may be a better fit in another position within the company.

5. **Celebrate Wins (Big and Small):**

   Acknowledge your team's hard work and successes, no matter how small. It's amazing how far a simple "thank you" can go in building loyalty and morale.

The Takeaway

Hiring the right team is one of the hardest things you'll do as an entrepreneur. It's messy, unpredictable, and full of bullshit. But it's also one of the most rewarding. When you finally assemble a team that clicks—one that believes in your vision and has the skills to execute it—you'll wonder how you ever survived without them.

So embrace the chaos, learn from your mistakes, and remember: you're not just hiring employees, you're building a foundation for your company's future. Don't rush it, don't settle, and don't let the bullshit get you down. In the end, it's worth it.

"Lots of people want to ride with you in the limo, but what you want is someone who will take the bus with you when the limo breaks down." - **Oprah Winfrey, Chairwoman/CEO of Harpo Productions and the Oprah Winfrey Network**

Chapter 10: Burnout—The Business Bullshit That Will Break You If You Let It

Burnout is the silent killer of businesses, and it's an insidious form of bullshit that sneaks up on you when you least expect it. It doesn't care how passionate you are, how much you love your company, or how badly you want to succeed. If you don't deal with it, burnout will break you—mentally, physically, and emotionally.

In this chapter, I'm going to get real about what burnout looks like, how to spot it before it consumes you, and, most importantly, how to fight back. Because trust me, you're going to need a plan.

How to Spot the Signs of Burnout

Burnout doesn't always look like the stereotypical image of someone curled up in the fetal position, crying in a dark room. It's much sneakier than that. Here are some of the warning signs I've experienced (and ignored) over the years:

1. **Constant Exhaustion:**

   You're tired all the time, no matter how much sleep you get. Even small tasks feel overwhelming.

2. **Irritability:**

   You find yourself snapping at people over minor things— your team, your family, even the barista who got your coffee order wrong.

3. **Loss of Passion:**

   The work that used to excite you now feels like a chore. You dread starting your day.

4. **Physical Symptoms:**

   Headaches, stomach issues, and other stress-related ailments become your new normal.

5. **Forgetfulness:**

   You start missing deadlines, forgetting meetings, or losing track of important details.

6. **Isolation:**

   You withdraw from friends and family because you're "too busy" or don't have the energy to engage.

If any of this sounds familiar, you're not alone. Burnout happens to the best of us. The key is recognizing it before it takes over your life.

The Bullshit That Fuels Burnout

Burnout doesn't happen in a vacuum. It's fueled by a toxic cocktail of unrealistic expectations, pressure to perform, and, yes, your own bullshit beliefs about work. Here are some of the biggest culprits:

1. **The Hustle Culture Trap:**

   We live in a world that glorifies the grind. "Rise and grind," "No days off," and "I'll sleep when I'm dead" are the mantras of hustle culture—and they're absolute garbage. Working yourself into the ground isn't noble; it's self-destructive.

2. **The "I Have to Do It All" Mentality:**

As a CEO or entrepreneur, it's easy to fall into the trap of thinking you have to do everything yourself. Delegation feels like weakness, and asking for help feels like failure. Spoiler alert: it's not.

3. **The Fear of Failure:**

Burnout often stems from a deep fear of letting people down—your investors, your team, your family. This fear drives you to overwork, even when it's not sustainable.

4. **Ignoring Boundaries:**

When you're constantly available—answering emails at midnight, taking calls on weekends—you're teaching people that your time isn't valuable. And that's a fast track to burnout.

How to Fight Back Against Burnout

The good news? Burnout isn't inevitable. You can fight back—if you're willing to change your mindset and your habits. Here's what's worked for me:

1. **Set Boundaries:**

Learn to say no. Protect your time and energy like your life depends on it—because it does. Stop answering emails after hours, take weekends off, and don't be afraid to delegate.

2. **Prioritize Self-Care:**

Exercise, eat well, and get enough sleep. I know it sounds

cliché, but it works. You can't pour from an empty cup.

3. **Take Breaks:**

   Step away from work regularly, even if it's just for a walk around the block. And for the love of all things holy, take a vacation. The world won't end if you're offline for a few days.

4. **Talk to Someone:**

   Whether it's a mentor, therapist, or fellow entrepreneur, don't keep your struggles bottled up. Sharing your feelings can help you process them and find solutions.

5. **Focus on What Matters:**

   Not everything on your to-do list is urgent. Learn to prioritize the tasks that move the needle and let go of the rest.

How I Deal with Burnout (and Try to Avoid It)

Over the years, I've picked up a few strategies for dealing with burnout. They're not magic pills, but they've saved my sanity more times than I can count.

1. Health is #1

When my three daughters were little, I would make my work schedule out every Sunday evening. The very first item was my workouts in the master schedule. Without my health, I cannot run my business, be a dad or a husband. I used to think breaks were for the weak. Now I know they're the secret weapon of anyone who wants to stay sane. Even a 10-minute walk outside can reset your brain and boost your energy.

2. Time Management

Time management is the backbone of running a successful business because, as a business owner, your time is your most valuable—and limited—resource. Every minute wasted is a missed opportunity to grow your business, serve your customers, or improve your bottom line. When you manage your time effectively, you're not just getting more done—you're focusing on the *right* things, the tasks that drive results and move your business forward. Without good time management, it's easy to get buried in distractions, lose focus, and end up working *in* your business instead of *on* it. Simply put, if you don't control your time, your time will control you—and your business will suffer for it. Day Timers if you want to keep a physical schedule or use your phone or table time management apps.

3. Learn to Say No

Here's some honest bullshit: as a business owner, you're going to feel like you have to say yes to everything. Every opportunity, every meeting, every request. But saying yes to everything is the fastest way to burn yourself out.

Now, I'm much more selective about where I spend my time and energy. If something doesn't align with my goals, I say no. Politely, but firmly. And honestly? It feels amazing.

4. Delegate Like Your Life Depends on It

Because, let's be real, it kind of does. For years, I tried to do everything myself. I thought, "If I want it done right, I have to do it." That's some Grade-A nonsense.

Delegating doesn't make you weak—it makes you smart. Whether it's hiring help, outsourcing tasks, or leaning on your team, you've got to let go of the stuff that's draining you. Focus on what you're best at and let others handle the rest.

5. Set Boundaries

Burnout loves to invade your personal life, so you've got to draw a line in the sand. For me, that means turning off email notifications after a certain time, not taking work calls on weekends, and carving out time for things I actually enjoy.

Boundaries aren't selfish—they're survival.

6. Make Self-Care Non-Negotiable

I used to roll my eyes at the term "self-care." I thought it was all bubble baths and overpriced candles. But now I get it. Self-care is about doing whatever keeps you sane, healthy, and happy.

For me, that means starting my mornings with a cup of coffee and a book instead of diving straight into work. It's a small ritual, but it sets the tone for my day and reminds me that I'm more than just a business owner.

The Business Bullshit of Burnout

Here's the truth: burnout is inevitable if you don't take care of yourself. It's not a matter of *if* it'll happen—it's *when*. And when it does, it's going to hit you harder than a tax audit.

So, take care of yourself. Take breaks, set boundaries, and don't be afraid to ask for help. Because at the end of the day, your business needs you to be at your best—not running on empty.

Arianna Huffington - *"Give up the delusion that burnout is the inevitable cost of success. Success isn't just about working hard, but working smart."*

Chapter 11: Setting Up Your Company – Corporation, LLC, or Sole Proprietor

Let's talk about one of the first big decisions you'll face as an entrepreneur—how to set up your company. Are you going to be a sole proprietor, an LLC, or a corporation? Sounds simple, right? Wrong. This is one of those sneaky bits of business bullshit that can trip you up before you even get out of the gate.

When I started my first business, I thought this would be a quick decision. Just pick a structure, fill out some forms, and boom— you're in business. But as I dug into it, I realized there's a lot more to it than meets the eye. The choice you make here has real consequences for your taxes, liability, and even how you run your day-to-day operations.

The problem is no one gives you a straight answer about which structure is best. Your accountant will tell you one thing, your lawyer will tell you another, and the internet? Well, the internet will just confuse the hell out of you. Meanwhile, you're left trying to figure out what the hell "pass-through taxation" and "double taxation" actually mean.

So let's cut through the crap. Here's what you need to know about the different business structures, how they work, and why this is some of the business bullshit you'll have to deal with as an entrepreneur.

What lawyer do I hire for this? Hire a general law firm, one person shops, to set up these entities. No need to hire a medium or large law firm for this area.

Sole Proprietor – The One-Man Show

If you're just starting out and want to keep things simple, a sole proprietorship is the most basic option. It's just you, running the show. No fancy paperwork, no legal hoops to jump through. You're the business, and the business is you.

The Good:

- **Easy to Set Up**. You don't need to file a bunch of paperwork or pay hefty fees. Just start doing business, and you're good to go.

- **Low Cost.** Since there's no complicated setup, you're not shelling out a ton of money upfront.

- **Full Control.** You make all the decisions—no partners, no board of directors, no one else to answer to.

The Bad:

- **Unlimited Liability.** This is the big one. If someone sues your business, they're suing *you*. Your personal assets—your house, your car, your savings—are all on the line. One lawsuit, and you could lose everything.

- **Harder to Raise Money.** Investors and lenders don't love sole proprietorships because there's no legal separation between you and your business.

The Verdict:

A sole proprietorship works if you're starting small and don't plan on taking big risks. But if you want to grow—or protect yourself—you'll need to upgrade to something with more structure.

LLC – The Medium Option

The LLC (Limited Liability Company) is the middle ground between a sole proprietorship and a corporation. It's flexible, it's protective, and it's a favorite among small business owners for good reason.

The Good:

- **Limited Liability.** Unlike a sole proprietorship, an LLC separates your personal assets from your business. If your business gets sued, they can't come after your house or your car.

- **Pass-Through Taxation.** The LLC itself doesn't pay taxes. Instead, the profits and losses "pass through" to your personal tax return, which keeps things simple.

- **Flexible Management.** LLCs don't have the rigid structure of corporations. You can run things however you want.

The Bad:

- **Costs More to Set Up.** Depending on your state, you'll need to file articles of organization and pay fees to get started.

- **Annual Fees and Paperwork.** Most states require LLCs to file annual reports and pay renewal fees. It's not a ton of money, but it's still an extra hassle.

- **Not Great for Investors.** If you're planning to raise serious capital, an LLC can get tricky. Investors tend to prefer corporations because they're more structured.

The Verdict:

If you're serious about your business but don't want the complexity of a corporation, an LLC is a solid choice. It gives you protection and flexibility without all the corporate red tape.

Corporation – The Big Leagues

If you're dreaming of going public someday—or just want to look like a serious player—a corporation might be the way to go. But be warned: this option comes with a lot of rules, regulations, and, you guessed it, bullshit.

The Good:

- **Limited Liability.** Like an LLC, a corporation protects your personal assets. Your liability is limited to what you've invested in the company.

- **Easier to Raise Money.** Corporations can issue stock, which makes them more attractive to investors.

- **Perpetual Existence.** A corporation doesn't die when the owner does. It keeps going, which is great if you're planning to build something that lasts.

The Bad:

- **Double Taxation.** Here's the kicker. Corporations pay taxes on their profits, and then you pay taxes again when you take dividends. It's a double whammy that can eat into your earnings.

- **Complicated Setup.** Corporations require articles of incorporation, bylaws, and a board of directors. It's a lot of paperwork and legal fees.

- **Ongoing Requirements.** Annual meetings, detailed record-keeping, and corporate minutes are all part of the deal.

The Verdict:

A corporation is overkill for most small businesses, but if you're planning to scale big or attract investors, it might be worth the hassle. Just be ready for the extra work—and the extra costs.

The Bullshit You'll Deal With

Here's why this whole process is such a pain in the ass:

1. **It's Overwhelming.** If you're new to business, trying to understand all the legal and tax implications of each structure can feel like learning a foreign language.

2. **Everyone Has an Opinion.** Your accountant will say one thing, your lawyer will say another, and your buddy who runs a landscaping business will swear by whatever worked for him.

3. **It's Not One-Size-Fits-All.** What works for someone else might not work for you. Your decision depends on your industry, your goals, and how much risk you're willing to take.

How to Make the Right Choice

So how do you cut through the noise and pick the right structure? Here's my advice:

1. **Start with Your Goals.** Are you trying to keep things small and simple, or are you planning to scale up? Your long-term vision should guide your decision.

2. **Talk to Professionals.** Don't try to figure this out on your own. Sit down with an accountant and a lawyer who specializes in small businesses. Yes, it'll cost you, but it's

worth it to start off on the right foot.

3. **Think About Liability.** If your business has any level of risk—whether it's client lawsuits, accidents, or debt—you'll want the protection of an LLC or corporation.

4. **Consider Taxes.** Taxes can make or break you. Make sure you understand the tax implications of your decision before you commit.

The Bottom Line

So take the time to do it right. Do your homework, get professional advice, and don't let the business bullshit overwhelm you. Because once you've got this part locked down, you can focus on what really matters—building your business and kicking ass.'

"I'm not a businessman, I'm a Business, man..." - Jay Z

Chapter 12: Negative Social Media Review

Ah, bad reviews—the digital punch to the gut. One moment, you're sipping your coffee, scrolling through social media, and feeling like you've got this whole business thing figured out. The next, BAM! A scathing comment or one-star review pops up that feels like it was written for the sole purpose of ruining your day. Worse, it's public. And in today's world, it's the modern-day equivalent of someone standing on a rooftop with a megaphone, shouting, "This company sucks!"

My first bad review hit me like a sucker punch. I reread the comment at least ten times, each word cut deeper than the last. My first instinct? Defend myself. Correct them. Prove the world that they were wrong. But over time, I learned that a bad review doesn't have to be a death sentence. In fact, if you handle it well, it can become an opportunity to showcase your professionalism, humanity, and resilience.

Let me walk you through what I've learned about dealing with bad social media reviews—the mistakes I've made, the lessons I've learned, and how to turn what feels like a disaster into a chance to shine.

The Reality of Bad Reviews

Here's the thing: bad reviews are inevitable. No matter how great your product or service is, you're going to piss someone off eventually. Maybe it's a genuine mistake on your part. Maybe it's a misunderstanding. Or maybe it's complete nonsense written by someone who's never even interacted with your business. (Yes, that happens more often than you'd think.)

The point is, bad reviews aren't always fair, but they're always public. And in the world of social media, where one bad review can spread like wildfire, how you handle it matters just as much—if not more—than the review itself.

What NOT to Do

Before we dive into the right way to handle bad reviews, let's talk about the things you absolutely should NOT do. Trust me, I've made these mistakes, and they only make things worse.

1. **Don't Respond in Anger**

   My first instinct when I got my first bad review was to fight back. I wanted to defend myself, explain why the reviewer was wrong, and show them (and everyone else) that they didn't know what they were talking about. Big mistake.
   Responding in anger makes you look defensive and unprofessional. Remember, your response isn't just for the reviewer—it's for everyone who's watching. Take a breath, take a walk, or scream into a pillow—but don't reply until you've had time to cool down.

2. **Don't Ignore It**

   Ignoring a bad review might feel like the easiest option, but it's a bad move. Social media is public, and silence can come across as indifference or even guilt. People notice when businesses don't respond, and it can hurt your reputation more than the review itself. However, Once, after speaking with my team, I chose to ignore this bad review. Why, because he was crazy and if I respond, he would have another chance to leave another insane bad remark.

3. **Don't Get Defensive**

I once saw a business owner reply to a bad review with, "Maybe if you weren't so impatient, you would've had a better experience." Yikes. That kind of response doesn't just make you look bad—it validates the reviewer's complaint. No matter how unfair the review feels, don't let your emotions get the best of you.

How to Handle a Bad Review the Right Way

Over the years, I've developed a simple system for dealing with bad reviews. It's not rocket science, but it works.

1. Pause and Reflect

Before you do anything, take a deep breath. A bad review feels personal, but it's not. It's feedback—sometimes exaggerated, sometimes unfair, but feedback nonetheless. Give yourself time to process your emotions before you respond.

2. Assess the Review

Not all bad reviews are created equal. Some are legitimate complaints, while others are just someone having a bad day. Ask yourself:

- Is there a valid issue here?

- Could we have handled this situation better?

- Or is this just someone venting with no real basis?

Understanding the nature of the review will help you craft a more effective response.

3. Respond Publicly (and Professionally)

Your response isn't just for the person who left the review—it's for everyone who sees it. This is your chance to show customers (and potential customers) that you care about feedback and are committed to improvement.

Here's my go-to formula for responding:

- **Thank them for their feedback.**

  Example: "Hi [Name], thank you for taking the time to share your thoughts."

- **Acknowledge their experience.**

  Example: "I'm sorry to hear that we didn't meet your expectations."

- **Offer to make it right.**

  Example: "We'd love the chance to resolve this issue. Please feel free to reach out to me directly at [email/phone]."

Example response:

"Hi [Name], thank you for bringing this to our attention. We're so sorry to hear about your experience and would love the opportunity to make things right. Please contact me directly at [email/phone], and we'll do our best to resolve this for you."

4. Take the Conversation Offline

Whenever possible, move the conversation out of the public eye. Not only does this show that you're serious about addressing the issue, but it also prevents any further drama from playing out in the comments section.

5. Learn from the Feedback

Every bad review is an opportunity to improve. Was there a legitimate issue with your product, service, or process? If so, fix it. Use the feedback to train your team, refine your systems, and prevent similar issues in the future.

Damage Control: When the Review Is False

Now, let's talk about the reviews that are completely false. Maybe it's a troll, a competitor, or someone who's just looking to stir up trouble. Here's how I handle those situations:

1. **Flag the Review**

   Most platforms (Google, Yelp, Facebook) allow you to flag reviews that violate their policies. Get your staff, family, or friends to flag it as well—it increases the chance of it being removed.

2. **Bury It with Positivity**

   If the platform won't remove the review (and let's be honest, they rarely do), the best way to fight back is to flood your page with positive reviews. Reach out to your happy customers and ask them to share their experiences. A few glowing five-star reviews will quickly bury the bad one.

Why Bad Reviews Are Just Another Part of the Business Bullshit

Bad reviews suck. They're frustrating, sometimes unfair, and always public. But they're also inevitable. No matter how great your product or service is, you'll never make everyone happy. And that's okay.

The trick is to handle bad reviews with intelligent thought-out plan. Take a breath, respond professionally, and use the feedback to get better. Because at the end of the day, a bad review isn't the end of the world—it's just another challenge to overcome. And in business, challenges are just part of the game.

"In every position that I've been in, there have been naysayers who don't believe I can do the work. And I feel a special responsibility to prove them wrong." **– Sonia Sotomayor (Supreme Court Justice)**

Chapter 13: Time Management –The Key to Achieve Success Quicker

If there's one thing every CEO or entrepreneur wishes they had more of, it's time. Not money, not talent—time. Because without time, none of the other things matter. You can have the best ideas, the most talented team, and all the funding in the world, but if you're wasting time on the wrong things, you'll never get anywhere.

Here's the kicker: time is the one thing you can't buy, borrow, or make more of. It's a finite resource, and once it's gone, it's gone. That's why time management isn't just a nice-to-have skill, it's the difference between success and failure. And yet, for all its importance, time management is one of the most misunderstood and overlooked aspects of running a business.

Over the years, I've learned—through trial, error, and a lot of frustration—that managing your time effectively isn't about working harder or longer. It's about working smarter.

Let me walk you through the bullshit of time management: the traps, the myths, and the strategies that have helped me regain control of my time and, ultimately, my life.

The Bullshit Myths About Time Management

Before we dive into the solutions, let's tackle some of the biggest myths about time management. These are the lies we tell ourselves, the excuses we use, and the traps that keep us stuck.

1. **"I'm Too Busy to Plan My Time."**

   This is the classic excuse. You're so busy doing the work that you don't have time to step back and figure out if you're even working on the right things. But here's the truth: if you don't make time to plan, you'll waste time later fixing your mistakes.

2. **"Multitasking Makes Me More Productive."**

Multitasking is one of the biggest lies of modern business. When you try to do multiple things at once, you're not being productive—you're being distracted. Studies show that multitasking actually reduces efficiency and increases mistakes. Focus on one thing at a time, and you'll get it done faster and better.

3. **"I'll Be More Productive If I Work Longer Hours."**

I bought into this myth for years. I'd work 12, 14, even 16-hour days, thinking I was out-hustling everyone else. But the reality is, long hours don't equal productivity. They equal burnout. Success isn't about how many hours you work; it's about how effectively you use those hours.

4. **"I'll Get to It Later."**

Procrastination is the silent killer of time management. Every time you put something off, you're borrowing time from your future self—and trust me, your future self isn't going to be happy about it.

The Time Management Bullshit You'll Face

Even if you have the best intentions, the world is full of time-wasters and distractions that will pull you off course. Here are some of the biggest culprits:

1. **The Endless Emails:**

   Your inbox is a black hole that will swallow your day if you let it. Every time you stop to check your email, you're breaking your focus and losing momentum.

2. **The "Can I Just Have a Minute?" People:**

   Whether it's a team member, a client, or a friend, there will always be people who interrupt you with "just a quick question." Those minutes add up, and before you know it, half your day is gone.

3. **The Meetings That Could've Been Emails:**

   Nothing wastes time like a poorly planned meeting. If you're spending more time in meetings than actually getting work done, something's wrong.

4. **The Social Media Rabbit Hole:**

   You tell yourself you're just going to check LinkedIn for five minutes, and an hour later, you're watching videos of cats playing the piano. Social media is a productivity killer, plain and simple.

How I Learned to Master My Time

I've developed a system that works (most of the time). Here's what's helped me the most:

1. Prioritize Like Your Life Depends on It

Not all tasks are created equal. Some move the needle, and others are just busywork. Every morning, I make a list of the top three things I need to accomplish that day—my "big rocks." If I get those three things done, I consider the day a success.

Tip: Use the Eisenhower Matrix to prioritize your tasks. Divide them into four categories:

- Urgent and Important: Do these first.

- Important but Not Urgent: Schedule these.

- Urgent but Not Important: Delegate these.

- Neither Urgent nor Important: Eliminate these.

2. Time Block Your Day

Time blocking has been a game-changer for me. Instead of letting my day be dictated by random interruptions, I schedule specific blocks of time for specific tasks. For example:

- 8–9 a.m.: Emails and admin tasks.

- 9–11 a.m.: Deep work (no distractions).

- 11–12 p.m.: Team check-ins.

- 1–3 p.m.: Client calls.

- 3–5 p.m.: Strategy and planning.

By assigning tasks to specific time slots, I stay focused and avoid jumping from one thing to another.

3. Learn to Say No

This was a tough one for me. As an entrepreneur, you want to say yes to every opportunity, every client, every meeting. But saying yes to everything means saying no to the things that really matter. I've learned to protect my time by saying no to anything that doesn't align with my priorities.

4. Delegate and Automate

You can't do everything yourself—and you shouldn't. Delegate tasks to your team, and use tools and software to automate repetitive tasks. Your time is too valuable to spend on things that someone (or something) else can do.

5. Take Breaks

This might sound counterintuitive, but taking breaks actually makes you more productive. Your brain needs time to rest and recharge. Step away from your desk, go for a walk, or just take five minutes to breathe. You'll come back more focused and energized.

The Takeaway

Remember, your time is your most valuable asset. Protect it, use it wisely, and don't let the bullshit steal it from you. Because at the end of the day, the way you manage your time will determine how quickly—and how successfully—you achieve your goals.

"If you want to make good use of your time, you've got to know what's most important and then give it all you've got." - **Lee Iacocca**

Chapter 14: Roller Coaster of Running Your Own Business

Running your own business is a lot like riding a roller coaster. At first, it seems thrilling—exciting even. You're at the top of the world, looking ahead at all the possibilities, filled with adrenaline and optimism. But before you know it, you're plummeting downhill, holding on for dear life, wondering if this was the worst decision you've ever made. One moment, you're celebrating a big win, and the next, you're drowning in a sea of unexpected problems, trying to stay afloat.

No one really warns you about the emotional whiplash of entrepreneurship. Sure, people talk about hard work, the long hours, and the risks, but no one tells you that running a business will test every part of your patience, your resilience, your confidence, and your sanity.

Let me take you through the highs, the lows, and the bullshit you'll inevitably encounter on this wild ride. Because if you're going to survive the roller coaster of running a business, you'd better know what to expect.

The Highs: Why We Do This Crazy Thing

Let's start with the good stuff, because there's a reason, we put ourselves through this madness. The heights of running your own business are unlike anything else.

1. **The Rush of Success**

   There's no feeling quite like landing that first big client, closing a deal you didn't think was possible, or seeing your idea come to life. It's like a shot of pure adrenaline, and it reminds you why you started in the first place.

2. **Freedom to Call the Shots**

One of the best parts of running your own business is the freedom it gives you. You get to make the decisions, set your own schedule, and create something that's truly yours. No boss, no bureaucracy—just you and your vision.

3. **The Sense of Accomplishment**

When you build something from nothing, it changes you. Every milestone, no matter how small, feels like a personal victory. You're not just working for a paycheck—you're building a legacy.

4. **The Impact You Make**

Whether it's creating jobs, solving a problem, or making someone's life easier, running a business gives you the opportunity to make a real impact. And that's something worth celebrating.

The Lows: The Gut Punches No One Warns You About

Of course, for every high, there's an equal (or sometimes greater) low. And let me tell you, the lows of running a business can hit you like a freight train.

1. **The Financial Stress**

There's no sugarcoating this: money will keep you up at night. Whether it's cash flow issues, unexpected expenses, or the constant pressure to hit revenue targets, financial stress is part of the game.

I'll never forget the time I had to dip into my personal savings just to make payroll. This was a harsh reminder that running a business is rarely smooth sailing.

2. **The Loneliness**

No one talks about how lonely entrepreneurship can be. Even if you have a team, the weight of responsibility falls squarely on your shoulders. When things go wrong, you can't complain to your employees, your clients, or even your friends—because they just don't get it.

3. **The Constant Pressure**

There's no clocking out when you run your own business. Even when you're "off," your brain is still running through to-do lists, solving problems, and worrying about what's next. The pressure is relentless, and it can feel like there's no escape.

4. **The Unexpected Bullshit**

No matter how well you plan, there will always be surprises—and not the good kind. Whether it's a sudden market shift, a key employee quits, or a client refusing to pay, the unexpected is a constant companion in business.

The Emotional Whiplash

The hardest part of running a business isn't the work—it's the emotional roller coaster. One minute, you're on top of the world, and the next, you're questioning every decision you've ever made.

I've had days where I've celebrated a huge win in the morning, only to get blindsided by a major setback in the afternoon. It's disorienting, and if you're not careful, it can wear you down.

Here's the truth: running a business will test your resilience in ways you can't imagine. It will force you to confront your fears, adapt to change, and keep going even when the odds are stacked against you.

How to Stay on the Roller Coaster Without Losing Your Mind

So, how do I survive the ups and downs of running my own business? Here's what's worked for me:

1. **Celebrate the Wins**

   When you're in the thick of it, it's easy to focus on what's going wrong and forget about what's going right. Take the time to celebrate your wins, no matter how small. They're what keep you going.

2. **Embrace the Chaos**

   "Roll with the Punches". Accept that there will be highs and lows, and try not to allow the bad days overshadow the good ones.

3. **Build a Support System**

You can't do this alone. Surround yourself with people who understand what you're going through—mentors, fellow entrepreneurs, or even a therapist. Having someone to talk to can make all the difference.

4. **Take Care of Yourself**

This is a tough one, especially when you're in hustle mode, but it's critical. Get enough sleep, eat well, exercise, and take breaks. You can't pour from an empty cup, and burnout is real.

5. **Keep the Big Picture in Mind**

When you're dealing with day-to-day bullshit, it's easy to lose sight of why you started in the first place. Remind yourself of your goals, your vision, and the impact you want to make. That's what will keep you going when the ride gets rough.

The Takeaway

Running your own business is not for the faint of heart, and it's definitely not for people who want stability or a clear path forward.

But if you can weather the highs and lows, if you can embrace the chaos and keep pushing forward, the ride is worth it. Because at the end of the day, the roller coaster of running a business isn't just about the destination—it's about the journey.

"I don't like to lose — at anything — yet, I've grown most not from victories, but setbacks." - **Serena Williams, tennis icon and founder of Serena Ventures**

Chapter 15: Vendors – The Art of Keeping a Great Working Relationship

In the business world: your vendors can make or break your company. Whether it's the supplier who keeps your shelves stocked, the software company powering your operations, or the freelancer designing your marketing materials, vendors are a critical piece of your success.

But here's the thing—they're also one of the biggest sources of business bullshit you'll ever encounter. Late deliveries, missed deadlines, miscommunications, price hikes, and outright incompetence are just a few of the joys you'll experience when dealing with vendors. And when things go wrong (and they will), it's your business—not theirs—that takes the hit.

Over the years, I've learned that managing vendor relationships is as much an art as it is a skill. It's not just about finding the best deal or the highest-rated supplier, it's about building a relationship that works for both sides. Finding a vendor who appreciates your business and always has your back.

The Vendor Bullshit You'll Encounter

Let's start with the ugly truth: working with vendors can be a minefield. Even the best vendors can sometimes drop the ball, and the worst ones can feel like they're actively sabotaging your business. Here's some of the bullshit you're likely to face:

1. **The Over-Promiser**

   This is the vendor who tells you exactly what you want to hear—"We can absolutely meet that deadline!" or "We guarantee the highest quality!"—only to under-deliver when it matters most. Their promises are big, but their follow-through is small.

2. The Ghoster

Need an update on your order? Too bad, because this vendor has disappeared into thin air. Emails go unanswered, calls go straight to voicemail, and you're left wondering if they're still in business.

3. The Price Gouger

Everything starts off fine—reasonable pricing, great service—but then, out of nowhere, they hit you with a price increase or hidden fees. Suddenly, you're paying way more than you budgeted for.

4. The Blame Shifter

When something goes wrong, this vendor is quick to point fingers. It's never their fault—it's yours, your team's, or some third party's. Accountability? Not in their vocabulary.

5. The "Good Enough" Vendor

This one doesn't actively screw things up, but they don't go above and beyond, either. They do the bare minimum to keep the relationship alive, and you're constantly left wondering if you could do better.

The Art of Building a Great Vendor Relationship

Now that we've covered the bullshit, let's talk about how to navigate it. A great vendor relationship doesn't just happen, it's something you have to work on, just like any other relationship. Here's what I've learned:

1. Start with the Right Fit

The foundation of a great vendor relationship is finding the right partner in the first place. This means doing your homework:

- Ask for References: Don't just take their word for it—talk to other businesses they've worked with.

- Check Their Track Record: Look for reviews, case studies, or testimonials.

- Align on Values: If your business values transparency, reliability, and quality, make sure your vendor does too.

Remember, the cheapest option isn't always the best. A vendor who delivers on time and meets your standards is worth their weight in gold.

2. Set Clear Expectations

One of the biggest causes of vendor bullshit is miscommunication. Avoid this by being crystal clear about your expectations from the start. This includes:

- Deadlines: Be specific about when you need things done, and build in some buffer time for unexpected delays.

- Standards: Define what "quality" means for your business. Don't assume they'll just know.

- Communication: Agree on how often you'll check in and the best way to reach each other.

Pro tip: Put everything in writing. Contracts, emails, and detailed agreements can save you a lot of headaches down the line.

3. Pay on Time

You'd be amazed at how far paying your vendors on time (or even early) can go in building goodwill. Vendors are running their own businesses, and cash flow is just as important to them as it is to you. A reputation as a reliable payer can make them more willing to go the extra mile for you when it matters.

4. Communicate Regularly

Don't just check in when there's a problem—stay in touch regularly to build a strong working relationship. This could be as simple as a monthly email to touch base or a quick phone call to discuss upcoming projects.

Communication is a two-way street, so make sure you're also listening to their concerns. If they're struggling with something on their end, work together to find a solution.

5. Treat Them Like Partners, Not Vendors

The best vendor relationships feel more like partnerships. When you treat your vendors with respect, involve them in your planning, and show appreciation for their work, they're more likely to reciprocate with loyalty and effort.

Example: If you're launching a new product, bring your vendor into the loop early. Share your goals and timelines so they can plan accordingly.

Dealing with Vendor Bullshit

Even with the best intentions, things will go wrong. Here's how to handle vendor issues without burning bridges:

1. Address Problems Quickly

Don't let small issues fester into big ones. If something isn't working, address it right away. Be specific about the problem and what you need to see changed.

2. Stay Calm and Professional

When a vendor screws up, it's tempting to let your frustration boil over. But yelling or being rude won't solve the problem—it'll just make them less motivated to work with you. Stay calm, stick to the facts, and focus on finding a solution.

3. Know When to Walk Away

Some vendor relationships just aren't worth saving. If a vendor repeatedly fails to meet your expectations, doesn't take accountability, or causes more stress than they're worth, it's time to cut ties. Have a backup plan in place so you're not left scrambling.

The Takeaway

The key is to treat your vendors like partners, communicate clearly, and address issues head-on. And when you inevitably run into vendor bullshit, don't let it throw you off course. Handle it with professionalism, learn from the experience, and focus on building strong, reliable partnerships that help your business thrive.

Because at the end of the day, your vendors aren't just suppliers, they're part of your team. And when they succeed, you succeed.

"The only way to deal with fear that I found in my life is a couple of ways one of those ways is to turn it on itself and ask yourself what am I afraid of?" - **Tony Robbins, motivation speaker**

Chapter 16: Cash Flow

"Never take your eyes off the cash flow because it's the lifeblood of business." - **Richard Branson**

Here's the brutal truth about cash flow: it's not just about raking in revenue. It's about making sure that money hits your account before your bills are due. Because as much as I'd love to pay my employees and landlords with IOUs and good vibes, "I'll get you next week" isn't an acceptable form of currency.

I will discuss all the angles of cash flow. Over the years, two key processed were implemented into my company to minimize cash flow "lows".

1. Invoicing quickly and follow through on collecting timely

2. Payments terms friendly to my company anticipating early material and labor bills that if not accounted for, could bring cash flow very quickly into the negative.

The Cash Flow Balancing Act

Managing cash flow is like refereeing to a never-ending fight between what's coming in and what's going out. Your job is to make sure expenses don't knock out income before the bell rings. Here's how I've learned to keep the chaos under control:

1. Get Paid Faster

The biggest headache with cash flow is the waiting game. You're stuck waiting for clients to pay their invoices, while your bills are due yesterday. Here's how I've learned to close the gap:

- Set Clear Payment Terms. Spell it out in your contracts. "Net 15" or "payment due upon receipt" leaves no room for confusion—or excuses.

- Payment Terms Determination. Know the cost of the job you just sold. If material costs are larger than the labor and you have to purchase the materials first, make sure your payment terms reflect that to keep your cash flow in the positive with higher payment first and smaller at the end. Please explain this to your customer also they understand— very important.

- Invoice Immediately. The faster you send the invoice, the faster you'll get paid. Procrastination here is a rookie mistake.

- Offer Incentives for Early Payment. A small discount for paying early can do wonders. It's amazing how fast people move when there's money to save.

---

2. Delay Payments (Without Burning Bridges)

On the flip side, I've learned to stretch out my outgoing payments when I can. Some vendors are open to negotiating longer payment terms—like 30 or even 60 days. The key is not to abuse it. If you push too hard, you'll end up on their blacklist faster than you can say "past due."

3. Try to Build a Cash Cushion by opening a 2nd business account and transferring 20 % of every receivable for emergencies.

I aim to keep at least three months' worth of operating expenses in reserve. It's not always easy, especially in the early days, but it's worth the effort. That cushion buys you time, and in this game, time is everything.

4. Forecast Like Your Life Depends on It

When I first started, I thought cash flow forecasting was for big corporations with CFOs and fancy accounting software. Wrong. Knowing what's coming in, what's going out, and when is critical for any business.

Now, I use a simple spreadsheet to map out my income and expenses for the next few months. It's not glamorous, but it works. And it keeps me from being blindsided by unexpected expenses—or worse, running out of money when I need it most.

5. Don't Be Afraid to Ask for Help

When cash flow gets tight, it's easy to fall into the trap of thinking you have to figure it out alone. But sometimes, asking for help is the smartest move.

Whether it's negotiating payment terms with a vendor, asking a client for an advance, or even taking out a short-term loan, you've got options. Just make sure you've got a plan to pay it back. Desperation without a strategy is how you dig yourself into a deeper hole.

The Reality of Cash Flow Bullshit

Cash flow isn't sexy, but it's one of the most important things you'll deal with as a business owner. It's also a never-ending source of stress. The key is to stay on top of it, plan ahead, and be ready to adapt when things go sideways.

Here's the truth: cash flow problems don't mean you're failing. They're just part of the business bullshit you signed up for. As long as you keep learning, keep hustling, and keep finding creative ways to make it work, you'll survive.

Because at the end of the day, cash flow isn't just about money— it's about keeping your business alive. And as much as it sucks to deal with, there's no better feeling than knowing you've got the grit to handle it.

Peter Drucker: *"Entrepreneurs believe that profit is what matters most in a new enterprise. But profit is secondary. Cash flow matters most," according to Cashbook*

Chapter 17: Problem Solving – The Key to Getting Your Company to the Next Level

Here's a hard truth about running a business that no one really prepares you for: your success isn't going to come from smooth sailing or perfectly executed plans. It's going to come from how you handle the bullshit—those unexpected, messy, frustrating problems that pop up when you least expect them.

Every time my company has hit a new level of success, it wasn't because everything went right. It was because something went wrong, and I figured out how to solve it. Problem-solving is the unglamorous, behind-the-scenes work that separates the businesses that thrive from the ones that fall apart.

Let me tell you something: no matter how good you are at planning, no matter how airtight your strategy is, shit will go wrong. A key client will back out. A vendor will drop the ball. Your best employee might quit with zero notice. And when that happens, you have two choices:

1. Panic and let the problem derail you.

2. Roll up your sleeves, figure it out, and come out stronger on the other side.

The second option isn't easy, but it's the only way forward. Let me take you through what I've learned about problem-solving—the mindset, the process, and why every problem is actually an opportunity in disguise.

Why Problem Solving Matters More Than You Think

If you're in business long enough, you'll realize something important: every level of success comes with a new set of problems.

When you're just starting out, your problems are small but urgent— how to get your first customer, how to stretch a tiny budget, how to keep the lights on. As you grow, the problems get bigger—and more complex. Now you're dealing with cash flow issues, scaling operations, managing a team, and staying ahead of competitors.

But here's the thing: problems are proof that you're doing something right. If you're not running into challenges, you're probably not pushing yourself or your business hard enough. The key isn't avoiding problems—it's learning how to solve them effectively.

The Bullshit of Problem Solving

Problem solving can be stressful, time-consuming, and often feels like you're putting out fires (I train my staff to NEVER say putting out fires—we must all learn to problem solve) instead of building your business. And the process is full of bullshit that can throw you off track:

1. **Take the Emotion out of the Equation**

   When a problem hits, your first instinct might be to panic. I've been there—heart racing, mind spinning, convinced that the sky is falling. But here's the truth: panic is the enemy of problem-solving. It clouds your judgment and makes everything feel worse than it actually is.

2. **The Blame Game**

Accountability is so important. Everyone on your team must be accountable. I also teach my team to never throw a teammate under the bus. This should always be done in private. When things go wrong, it's tempting to point fingers—at your team, your clients, your vendors, or even yourself. But blaming doesn't solve the problem. It's a distraction, and it wastes precious time you could be using to find a solution.

3. **The Quick Fix Trap**

Not every problem has an easy solution. Sometimes, you'll be tempted to slap a Band-Aid on a problem just to make it go away. But quick fixes often create bigger problems down the line. *I always train my team when they encounter a problem-solving dilemma, always take the quality route with materials and what is best for our customers*

How I Approach Problem Solving Now

Over the years, I've developed a system for tackling problems that works for me. It's not flashy, but it's effective. Here's how I approach problem-solving:

1. Pause and Breathe

When a problem hits, my first step is to pause. I know this sounds counterintuitive—after all, the instinct is to jump in and start fixing things. But taking a moment to breathe and clear your head is crucial. It helps you approach the problem with a level head instead of pure emotion.

2. Define the Problem

Before you can solve a problem, you need to understand it. What's actually happening? What's causing it? Who's affected? The clearer you are about the problem, the easier it is to find a solution.

Pro Tip: Avoid assumptions. Dig into the details and get the facts. I've wasted too much time solving the *wrong* problem because I didn't take the time to fully understand the situation.

3. Break It Down

Big problems can feel overwhelming, so I break them into smaller, manageable pieces. What's the first step I can take? What's the next? Tackling one piece at a time makes even the biggest problems feel less daunting.

4. Look for Opportunities

Here's the part most people miss: every problem is an opportunity in disguise. What can you learn from this situation? How can you turn it into a win? Some of my company's biggest breakthroughs came from problems that forced me to rethink my approach.

Example: We once lost a major client due to an internal communication breakdown. It was a gut punch, but it forced us to overhaul our processes and improve how we worked as a team. The result? We became more efficient, and it helped us land even bigger clients down the line.

5. Involve the Right People

You don't have to solve every problem alone. Bring your team, your advisors, or even an outside expert if needed. Different perspectives can lead to better solutions, and sharing the load makes the process less stressful.

6. Take Action

Once you have a plan, act on it. Don't overthink or second-guess yourself. Even if the solution isn't perfect, taking action moves you closer to solving the problem.

7. Reflect and Learn

After the dust has settled, I always take time to reflect. What caused the problem? What could we have done differently? And most importantly, how can we prevent it from happening again? Every problem is a chance to learn and improve.

The Mindset of a Problem Solver

Solving problems isn't just about having a process—it's about having the right mindset. Here's what I've learned about staying mentally tough when things go sideways:

1. **Embrace the Challenge**

   Instead of dreading problems; I've learned to see them as opportunities to grow. Every problem I solve makes me and my business stronger.

2. **Stay Positive**

   Negativity doesn't solve problems. When things get tough, I remind myself that every problem has a solution—it's just a matter of finding it.

3. **Focus on What You Can Control**

   Some problems are out of your hands. Instead of wasting energy on things you can't change, focus on what you *can* do to move forward.

The Takeaway

Problem-solving isn't just a skill—it's a mindset, a habit, and one of the most important tools in your entrepreneurial toolbox. When you approach problems with clarity, creativity, and determination, they stop being obstacles and start becoming opportunities.

"Don't limit yourself. Many people limit themselves to what they think they can do. You can go as far as your mind lets you. What you believe, remember, you can achieve." - **Albert Einstein**

Chapter 18: Celebrate the Wins for Your Company and Yourself

Let me ask you something: when was the last time you celebrated a win? And I'm not talking about a quick "Nice job" before diving headfirst into the next mountain of work. I mean truly celebrated paused, reflected, and gave yourself or your team the recognition you deserve.

If your answer is "I don't remember" or even worse, "I've never done that," then we need to talk.

Look, running a business is a grind. It's long nights, early mornings, endless fires to put out, and an ever-growing to-do list. You're constantly in motion, chasing the next goal, solving the latest problem, and trying to keep the wheels from falling off. And somewhere in all that chaos, you forget to celebrate the very thing you're working so damn hard for: success.

I get it because I used to be the same way. I'd hit a big milestone—something I'd been working toward for months—and instead of celebrating, I'd immediately move on to the next thing. It was like I was on an endless treadmill of achievement. There was always another goal, another deadline, another challenge to tackle.

But here's the thing: if you don't stop to celebrate your wins, what's the point? Life (and business) isn't just about getting shit done—it's about enjoying the journey. Celebrating the wins, both big and small, is how you recharge, stay motivated, and remind yourself why you started this whole crazy ride in the first place.

The "I Forgot to Celebrate" Moment

Let me take you back to one of the first big wins in my business. I'd just hit a major revenue goal—a number I'd dreamed about when I was first starting out. It was one of those "pinch me" moments, the kind of milestone that reminds you why all the late nights and early mornings are worth it.

And what did I do? Did I break out the champagne? Treat myself to something nice? It takes five minutes to soak it in?

Nope. I opened my laptop and started planning the next quarter's goals.

It wasn't until a friend called to congratulate me that I realized I hadn't even taken a second to acknowledge what I'd accomplished. "You need to celebrate this," she said. "You worked hard for it."

She was right. I had worked hard. And in my rush to move on to the next thing, I was missing the point entirely. That moment taught me an important lesson: celebrating your wins isn't optional—it's essential.

Why Celebrating Your Wins Matters

Celebrating your wins isn't just about feeling good (though let's be honest, that's a nice bonus). It's about staying connected to your purpose and keeping your energy and motivation alive. Here's why it matters:

1. **It Keeps You Motivated**

   Running a business is a marathon, not a sprint. Celebrating your wins gives you the energy to keep going, especially when the road gets rough.

2. **It Builds Confidence**

   Every win, no matter how small, is proof that you're capable of achieving your goals. Celebrating reinforces that confidence and reminds you that you're making progress.

3. **It's Good for Your Mental Health**

   Let's face it—being an entrepreneur is stressful. Celebrating your successes is a way to balance out the hard times and remind yourself that the grind is paying off.

4. **It Strengthens Your Team**

   If you've got a team, celebrating wins together fosters camaraderie and reinforces a sense of shared purpose. People want to feel like their work matters, and celebrating is a way to show them that it does.

Big Wins vs. Small Wins

Not every win has to be a major milestone to be worth celebrating. Sure, landing a big client or hitting a revenue goal is a big deal. But so are the smaller victories—the ones that might not seem like much on the surface but are just as important.

Here are some of the "small wins" I've learned to celebrate:

- Wrapping up a difficult project that took way longer than expected.

- Getting a glowing review from a happy customer.

- Solving a problem that had been hanging over my head for weeks.

- Making it through a Monday without spilling coffee on myself (hey, we take what we can get).

The point is progress is progress. Every step forward deserves recognition.

How I Celebrate Now

These days, I make it a point to celebrate my wins—both for my company and for myself. Here's how I do it:

1. Make It Personal

Celebrations don't have to be extravagant or expensive. The key is to do something that feels meaningful to you. For me, that might mean treating myself to my favorite dessert, taking a day off to relax, or buying a small gift as a reminder of the milestone.

2. Share the Joy

Celebrating is even sweeter when you share it with others. If it's a team win, I'll call a meeting and make sure everyone knows how much their hard work contributed to the success. For personal wins, I'll text a friend or family member and say, "Guess what I just accomplished?"

Pro tip: Share your wins with your customers and community, too. They love to see your success, and it builds goodwill.

3. Reflect on the Journey

Before I move on to the next goal, I take a moment to reflect on what I've achieved and how I got there. What worked? What didn't? What did I learn? Taking the time to appreciate the journey helps me stay grounded and grateful.

4. Get Silly

Not every celebration has to be serious. Sometimes, I'll crank up my favorite song and have a little dance party in my office. (Pro tip: Beyoncé is always a good choice.)

The Bullshit That Keeps You from Celebrating

If you're not celebrating your wins, chances are one of these bullshit excuses is getting in the way:

1. **"I Don't Have Time."**

   Here's the thing: you're never going to "find" time to celebrate. You have to make time. And trust me, it's worth it.

2. **"It's Not a Big Deal."**

   Every win is a big deal. Don't downplay your accomplishments just because they don't seem earth-shattering. Progress is progress.

3. **"I'll Celebrate When I Reach the Next Goal."**

   If you're always waiting for the "next" thing, you'll never stop to appreciate what you've already achieved. Celebrate now.

The Takeaway

Celebrating your wins is about more than just marking a moment—it's about giving yourself and your team the credit you deserve for all the hard work, determination, and resilience it took to get there.

So the next time you achieve something—whether it's landing a big client, solving a tricky problem, or just making it through a tough week—take a moment to celebrate. Throw a party, treat yourself, or just sit quietly and say, "I did that."

Because you did. And you deserve to enjoy it.

"Remember to celebrate milestones as you prepare for the road ahead." - **Nelson Mandela's** words remind us to acknowledge achievements as important markers in the journey toward future goals

Chapter 19: Litigation and Selecting the Right Attorney

When I started my business, I naively believed that litigation wouldn't be part of my journey. I had this idealistic vision where everything ran smoothly, contracts were honored, and everyone played fair. Spoiler alert: that's not how the real world works.

Here's the thing about running a business: no matter how much you plan, no matter how airtight your contracts are, and no matter how well you think you treat your clients or employees, at some point, legal trouble is going to come knocking. Maybe it's a disgruntled client, a former employee, or some random curveball you never saw coming. Whatever it is, it's not fun, and it's definitely not something you can ignore.

Why You Need the Right Attorney

Whether you're dealing with a lawsuit, drafting contracts, or trying to prevent legal problems before they start, having the right attorney on your team can make all the difference. Think of them as your insurance policy against the chaos of the legal world.

Here's the thing about attorneys: they're not just for dramatic courtroom battles or episodes of "Suits." A good attorney is like a bodyguard for your business. They're there to protect you, guide you, and—most importantly—keep you from accidentally making things worse.

How to Select the Right Attorney

Not all attorneys are created equal. Picking the wrong one can cost you time, money, and—worst of all—a favorable outcome. Here's what I've learned about finding the right attorney to represent your company:

1. Know What You Need

Before you start your search, figure out exactly what kind of help you need. Attorneys specialize in different areas:

- Contracts

- Employment law

- Intellectual property

- Litigation

In my case, I needed someone who specialized in small business litigation. I wasn't about to hire a generalist—I wanted someone who knew the ins and outs of my specific industry.

2. Choose the Right Firm

The size and focus of the law firm matter more than you think. Here's what I've learned:

- Go Medium-Sized: Medium firms have the resources to handle the grunt work at lower rates while still giving you personalized attention.

- Find a Specialist: Look for a firm that knows your industry inside and out. If they understand the nuances of your business, they'll be more effective—and save you money in the long run.

- Avoid Solo Practitioners: A one-person firm might seem cost-effective, but every task—big or small—will be billed at their hourly rate. That adds up fast.

- Be Wary of Giant Firms: At massive firms, you risk being just another number. Your case might not get the attention it deserves.

3. Ask for Recommendations

One of the best ways to find a great attorney is by asking other business owners. I called up a few people in my network and asked, "Who do you trust when it comes to legal issues?" Their recommendations were gold.

4. Interview Potential Attorneys

Once I had a shortlist, I set up meetings with each attorney. This wasn't just a formality—I used it as an opportunity to grill them. I asked:

- "Have you handled cases like mine before?"

- "What's your strategy for resolving disputes?"

- "How often will I hear from you?"

- "What are your fees, and what other costs should I expect?"

Their answers told me everything I needed to know about whether they were the right fit.

What My Attorney Taught Me

When I finally found the right attorney, it was a game-changer. They reviewed my case, laid out my options, and came up with a strategy to resolve the dispute as quickly and painlessly as possible.

Long story short, we ended up settling out of court. It wasn't fun, and it definitely wasn't cheap—but it was the best possible outcome. And the peace of mind I got from having a professional handle it? Absolutely priceless.

Lessons Learned from Litigation

My brush with litigation taught me a few hard but invaluable lessons:

1. Stay Calm

When legal trouble comes knocking, it's easy to panic. Don't. Take a deep breath, assess the situation, and remind yourself: you're not the first business owner to go through this, and you won't be the last.

2. Document Everything

The reason I was able to defend myself was because I had detailed records—contracts, emails, invoices, you name it. Keeping thorough documentation isn't just a good habit—it's your lifeline in a legal dispute.

3. Don't Be a Hero

Trying to handle legal issues on your own is a rookie mistake. You wouldn't try to perform surgery on yourself, so don't try to play as an attorney. Leave it to the professionals.

4. Be Clear About Your Stance

Do you want to settle? Go to trial? Just send a strongly worded letter. Make sure your attorney understands your goals from the start. A good attorney will tailor their strategy to align with what you want to achieve.

5. Learn from the Experience

Legal issues are stressful, but they're also a learning opportunity. After it's all said and done, take stock of what happened. What can you do differently to prevent this from happening again?

The Bottom Line

No one starts a business thinking they'll end up in litigation, but the reality is, it's a possibility you need to prepare for. The key is to stay calm, document everything, and—most importantly—find the right attorney to guide you through the process.

So, if you ever find yourself staring down a legal dispute, don't panic. Take a deep breath, pick up the phone, and remind yourself: you've got this. With the right attorney in your corner, you'll come out stronger on the other side.

"Discourage litigation. Persuade your neighbors to compromise whenever you can. Point out to them how the nominal winner is often a real loser—in fees, expenses, and waste of time."

Chapter 20: Unscrupulous Competitors – When the Gloves Come Off

Welcome to the world of unscrupulous competitors—a world where the gloves come off, and the rules don't seem to matter. If you've been in business long enough, you've probably encountered one of these shady characters. If you haven't yet, it's only a matter of time.

Let me paint a picture for you: you're working tirelessly to build your business. You're putting in the time, the energy, and the heart to create something you're proud of. Things are starting to fall into place, and then, out of nowhere, a competitor shows up and starts playing dirty.

Maybe they're undercutting your prices in ways that don't even make sense. Maybe they're spreading lies about your business or poaching your best employees. Maybe they're outright copying your ideas, branding, or products. Whatever it is, it feels personal.

But here's the thing: while dealing with unethical competitors is frustrating (and, let's be honest, infuriating), it's also a test of your resilience and resourcefulness. Let me take you through what I've learned about navigating this particular brand of business bullshit, staying true to your values, and coming out stronger on the other side.

The Bullshit You'll Face from Unscrupulous Competitors

First, let me break down some of the shady tactics you might encounter. These aren't just theoretical. I've experienced most of them firsthand, and I can tell you—they're as maddening as they sound.

1. Price Gouging

Some competitors will drop their prices so low it's impossible for you to compete without losing money. They're not playing the long game—they're trying to bleed you dry by making it impossible for you to stay profitable.

2. Spreading Lies

Whether it's whisper campaigns, fake reviews, or outright slander, some competitors will do whatever it takes to damage your reputation. It's dirty, it's petty, and it can be devastating if you're not prepared.

3. Copycatting

This one stings. You spend months (or years) creating something unique, only to have a competitor swoop in and copy your ideas, branding, or products. They're not innovating—they're stealing.

4. Employee Poaching

There's nothing worse than losing a key team member—unless it's losing them to a competitor who's deliberately targeting your talent.

5. Backdoor Deals

Some competitors will go behind your back to undercut you with vendors, partners, or clients. They'll offer deals that sound too good to be true, just to squeeze you out.

My First Encounter with an Unscrupulous Competitor

I'll never forget the first time I ran into one of these unethical players. We were doing well—gaining traction, building our reputation, and hitting our goals. Then, seemingly out of nowhere, a new competitor emerged.

At first, I didn't think much of it. Competition is part of the game, right? But it quickly became clear that this wasn't just competition, they were playing dirty.

They started offering absurdly low prices that we couldn't match without losing money. They spread rumors about our business that weren't even remotely true. And they even tried to lure away some of our employees. It felt like an all-out attack.

At first, I was furious. I wanted to fight fire with fire, but I quickly realized that stooping to their level wasn't the answer. Instead, I focused on protecting my business, doubling down on what made us unique, and finding ways to outsmart them without compromising my integrity.

How to Deal with Unscrupulous Competitors

If you're dealing with unethical competition, here's what I've learned about how to navigate the situation without losing your sanity—or your soul:

1. Keep Your Cool

The first thing you need to do is stay calm. When you're dealing with shady tactics, it's easy to let anger take over. But reacting emotionally can lead to bad decisions. Take a step back, assess the situation, and approach it strategically.

2. Focus on Your Strengths

One of the best ways to combat dirty competition is to double down on what makes your business unique. What do you offer that they can't replicate? Whether it's exceptional customer service, superior quality, or a loyal community, lean into your strengths.

3. Protect Your Reputation

If a competitor is spreading lies or fake reviews, you need to act quickly to protect your reputation. Respond professionally, provide evidence to refute false claims, and rally your supporters to share their positive experiences with your business.

4. Document Everything

If a competitor is crossing legal or ethical lines, make sure you're documenting everything. Screenshot fake reviews, save emails, and keep records of any suspicious activity. This will be invaluable if you need to take legal action.

5. Consider Legal Action (When Necessary)

Speaking of legal action, don't be afraid to consult an attorney if a competitor is engaging in outright theft or defamation. A cease-and-desist letter can be surprisingly effective at stopping bad behavior in its tracks.

6. Play the Long Game

Unscrupulous competitors often focus on short-term wins, but you're in this for the long haul. Stay consistent, keep delivering value, and trust that your reputation will outlast their dirty tactics.

7. Don't Fight Fire with Fire

It's tempting to stoop to their level and fight dirty, but trust me—that's a mistake. Not only does it compromise your integrity, but it can also damage your reputation in the long run. Stay above the fray and let your actions speak for themselves.

What Unscrupulous Competitors Have Taught Me

As much as I hate to admit it, dealing with dirty competitors has taught me some valuable lessons:

1. **Competition Makes You Stronger**

   Facing unethical competitors forced me to get better—better at communicating my value, better at protecting my business, and better at staying focused on my goals.

2. **Integrity Matters**

   At the end of the day, your reputation is everything. No matter how tempting it might be to fight dirty, staying true to your values is what will set you apart and earn you loyalty from customers and partners.

3. **Success Is the Best Revenge**

   The best way to deal with shady competitors? Beat them at their own game—not by playing dirty, but by building a business so strong, they can't touch you.

The Takeaway

The next time a competitor tries to play dirty, take a deep breath, stand tall, and remind yourself: you're better than that—and you'll prove it.

"If you mind your own business, you'll stay busy all the time." - **Hank Williams Jr.** To stay busy by minding your own business means focusing on personal tasks and objectives, disregarding distractions and external influences

Chapter 21: Making a Simple Idea a Reality

Every business starts with a spark—a moment of clarity where you think, *This is it. This is the idea that's going to change everything.* It feels exciting, almost magical, like you've discovered a secret no one else knows about.

But here's the reality: having an idea is the easy part. Turning that idea into a functioning, profitable business? That's where the grind begins. It's not just about passion or creativity—it's about execution. And execution is where most people get stuck, tripped up, or completely derailed.

Why? Because the process of taking a simple idea and making it real is full of obstacles, frustrations, and—let's be honest—a mountain of business bullshit no one warns you about.

So, if you've got an idea that's been keeping you up at night, let me walk you through the steps to bring it to life. These are the starting points you need to tackle *before* you go public. Get this right, and you're laying the foundation for success. Get these wrong, and you're setting yourself up for a world of headaches.

Step 1: Choose a Company Name

This sounds simple, right? Wrong. Picking a company name is one of those tasks that seems straightforward until you actually sit down to do it. Suddenly, every name you come up with is either taken, too generic, or just doesn't feel right.

Here's the trick: your name should be memorable, easy to spell, and give people an idea of what your business does. Avoid trendy buzzwords that will feel outdated in a few years. And for the love of everything holy, don't overthink it.

The Bullshit: You'll obsess over this more than you should. Don't let it paralyze you. A good name is important, but it's not the *only* thing that will make or break your business.

Step 2: Choose a Tagline

Your tagline is like a quick elevator pitch for your business. It's a short, punchy phrase that sums up what you do, IN THREE WORDS, and how you add value. Think "Just Do It" (Nike)

The Goal: Make it clear, concise, and compelling. It should make someone think, *I want to know more about this company.*

Step 3: Make Sure the Domain Name Is Available

This is where things can get frustrating. You might come up with the perfect name, only to find the domain is already taken—or worse, it's for sale at some ridiculous price.

Use tools like GoDaddy or Namecheap to search for available domains. Try variations if needed, but keep it simple and easy to remember. If your domain looks like a Scrabble board exploded (e.g., "MyCompany123.biz"), it's time to go back to the drawing board.

Pro Tip: Lock down your social media handles at the same time. Consistency across platforms is key to building a recognizable brand.

Step 4: Make Sure the Corporation Name Isn't Taken

Before you fall in love with your company name, check with your local Secretary of State's office to make sure it's not already registered. If it is, you'll have to come up with something else—or risk a legal battle later on, which is the kind of business bullshit you *don't* want to deal with.

Step 5: See If You Can Trademark the Name

A trademark (or patent, depending on your product) protects your brand from copycats. This step isn't mandatory right out of the gate, but if you're serious about scaling your business and building a recognizable brand, it's worth considering.

The Bullshit: Trademarks are expensive and time-consuming. You'll need to work with an attorney, file paperwork, and wait for months to hear back. But peace of mind is worth it if your business takes off.

Step 6: Build Your Website

Your website is your business's virtual storefront—it's often the first impression people will have of your brand. But here's the trap: don't spend thousands of dollars hiring a developer unless you absolutely have to.

Use platforms like Without Code, Squarespace, or Wix to build your site yourself. This way, you have full control and don't have to rely on a developer every time you need to make a small change. Trust me, waiting two weeks for someone to update your "About" page is the kind of frustration you don't need in your life.

Must-Haves for Your Website:

- A clear description of what you do.

- Movement

- Video

- Easy navigation.

- A way to contact you.

- Testimonials or case studies (if you have them).

- Hi Resolution pictures of your product

Step 7: Create a Brochure or Flyer

This brochure will be digital as well as physical. Yes, we live in a digital world, but physical marketing materials still have their place. A well-designed brochure or flyer can be a powerful tool when you're meeting potential clients in person.

Keep it simple—focus on your core value proposition and what makes your business unique. And don't skimp on the design. A cheap, poorly designed flyer screams "amateur."

Step 8: Determine Your Marketing Plan and Target Customers

This is where a lot of entrepreneurs get stuck. Who are your customers? How are you going to reach them? What's your marketing budget?

Start by defining your target audience. Be as specific as possible:

- Who are they?

- What age group?

- What net income?

- Where do they hang out online (or in the real world)?

Step 9: Social Media

Social media can be virtually free, if you work these platforms yourself:

- Instagram
- LinkedIn
- Twitter
- You Tube
- Facebook

Contact three companies that specialize in social media content and posting. Listen to their plan and price. $2,000-$3,000 a month is a starting point.

Then, figure out how to get in front of your "TARGET AUDIENCE".. Are you using social media ads? Email campaigns? Networking events? The more focused your marketing plan, the better your chances of success.

The Bullshit: Marketing is a never-ending process. Just when you think you've nailed it, trends change, algorithms shift, and you're back at square one. Be ready to adapt.

Step 10: Go Above and Beyond for The First 5 Customers

This is the most important step. Your first five customers are the foundation of your business. If you blow it with them, you're done. But if you turn them into raving fans, they'll become your best salespeople.

Go above and beyond to make sure they're thrilled with your product or service. Your best staff members, best products—make these first 5 special—whatever the cost—don't worry about making very much money on these first five. Overdeliver. Follow up. Ask for feedback. And when they're happy, ask them to leave a glowing review—or refer you to their friends.

Pro Tip: Word of mouth is still one of the most powerful marketing tools out there. Your first five customers can create a ripple effect that drives your next 10, 20, or 100 customers.

The Bullshit You'll Face Along the Way

Let's not sugarcoat it—this process isn't always smooth sailing. You'll deal with:

- Decision fatigue. You'll second-guess every choice, from your logo to your tagline to your pricing.

- Imposter syndrome. You'll wonder if you're qualified to do this—or if anyone will take you seriously.

- Setbacks. Your website will crash, your first flyer will look like crap, or your dream client will ghost you.

But here's the thing: every entrepreneur deals with this. The key is to push through, learn as you go, and keep your eyes on the prize.

The Bottom Line

I always felt that if you have a great product and people like/trust you—your company WILL BE successful and be around for years to come. And it's definitely not for the faint of heart. But if you're willing to put in the work, you can turn your spark of inspiration into something real, something tangible, and something that makes an impact.

So, stop waiting. Start small, take one step at a time, and don't let the bullshit scare you off. Because the only thing worse than failing is never trying at all.

"The future belongs to those who believe in the beauty of their dreams." - **Eleanor Roosevelt**

Chapter 22: The Art of Pitching – Convincing the World Your Idea Is Brilliant

The Art of Pitching aka Convincing the World Your Idea Is as Brilliant as You Think It Is

Pitching is one of those parts of entrepreneurship that no one warns you about. You can have the greatest idea in the world, the perfect product, the slickest branding—but if you can't pitch it, you're dead in the water. Investors, customers, partners, employees—they all need to buy in. And if your pitch falls flat, it doesn't matter how brilliant your idea is.

The real kicker? Pitching is full of business bullshit. You'll deal with skeptical faces, tough questions, and people who are *this close* to saying yes but end up ghosting you anyway. But if you can master the art of pitching, you'll unlock one of the most valuable skills an entrepreneur can have.

The Bullshit of Pitching

Before we dive into the strategies, let's get real about why pitching can be such a grind:

1. You're Putting Yourself Out There. Pitching is personal. You're not just selling an idea—you're selling yourself. And every time you hear "no," it stings.

2. People Don't Trust Easily. Everyone's been burned by bad products, shady companies, or empty promises. They're skeptical, and it's your job to break through that wall.

3. You Have to Think on Your Feet. Investors will grill you. Customers will ask tough questions. If you're not prepared, they'll see right through you.

4. Rejection is Inevitable. Not everyone will say yes—even if your pitch is flawless. And hearing "no" over and over again can mess with your confidence.

The Rules of Pitching Without the Bullshit

If you want to pitch like a pro, you need to follow a few simple—but crucial—rules. These aren't gimmicks or hacks. They're the foundation of a pitch that works.

1. Don't Sell — Inform and Educate

Here's where most people screw up: they try to sell, sell, sell. They bombard their audience with features, benefits, numbers, and flashy one-liners, thinking that will seal the deal. It won't.

What actually works? Informing and educating. When you focus on teaching your audience something valuable—about their problem, the market, or how your solution works—your pitch will sell itself.

Example:

Instead of saying, *"Our software is the best on the market, and here's why you should buy it,"* try:

"Here's what we've learned about the biggest challenges companies like yours face—and here's how we've solved those challenges for others."

When you educate, you position yourself as an expert. And people want to buy from experts.

2. Establish Relationships First

People don't buy from strangers. They buy from people they like, trust, and feel connected to. So, before you start pitching your idea, focus on building a relationship.

Ask yourself:

- Do they like me? If they don't like you, they're not going to care about your pitch. Smile, make small talk, and find common ground.

- Do they trust me? Trust takes time to build, but it starts with being authentic, honest, and genuinely interested in their needs.

- Do they see me as someone who can help them? Make it clear that you're here to solve their problem—not just make a sale.

Pro Tip: If you rush straight into your pitch without establishing a connection, you'll lose them before you even get started.

3. Always Ask, "What Can I Do to Help You?"

This is the simplest, most powerful question you can ask in any pitch: *"What can I do to help you?"*

Why? Because it shifts the focus from *you* to *them*. Instead of talking about your product or your company, you're showing that you care about their needs and are willing to go the extra mile to meet them.

And here's the thing: when you genuinely help someone—even in a small way—they'll remember it. That goodwill makes them far more likely to say yes when you ask for the sale.

4. Find Out What They Need

You can't pitch effectively if you don't know what your audience actually needs. So, before you dive into your presentation, ask questions.

- What are your biggest challenges right now?

- What's working for you, and what's not?

- What would a perfect solution look like to you?

When you understand their needs, you can tailor your pitch to show exactly how your idea solves their problem. And when they feel understood, they're far more likely to trust you.

5. Ask About Past Experiences

Here's a secret weapon: ask if they've had bad experiences with other companies in the past.

Why? Because it gives you insight into their pain points—and an opportunity to position yourself as the solution.

Example:

If they say, *"We worked with a company that overpromised and under-delivered,"* you can say, *"That's exactly why we're so focused on transparency and delivering measurable results."*

By addressing their past frustrations, you show that you're different—and that you actually care about meeting their expectations.

6. Always Ask to Get Hired

If you want someone to hire you, you have to ask. Be direct. Be confident. Don't dance around it.

Instead of saying, *"Let me know if you're interested,"* say:
"I'd love to work with you—what would it take to get started?"

Or even better:
"Is there any reason we can't move forward today?"

You're putting the ball in their court and making them tell you "no" if they're not ready. Most people won't say no outright—they'll tell you what they need to feel comfortable moving forward. And that's your chance to close the deal.

The Bullshit You'll Face

Pitching isn't all smooth sailing. Here's some of the nonsense you'll have to deal with:

1. **People Ghosting You.** You'll give a killer pitch, they'll seem excited, and then... radio silence. It happens. Follow up, but don't take it personally.

2. **Tough Questions.** Investors and customers will grill you. Be prepared to defend your idea without getting defensive.

3. **"Let Me Think About It."** This is the polite way of saying no. Push gently: *"What's holding you back from making a decision today?"*

4. **Rejection.** Some people just won't bite. Don't let it discourage you. Learn from it, refine your pitch, and move on.

The Bottom Line

The art of pitching isn't just about selling—it's about connecting, educating, and building trust. It's about showing people that you're not just another entrepreneur with a flashy idea—you're someone who can solve their problem and make their life better.

Will it be frustrating? Absolutely. Will you hear "no" more times than you can count? Definitely. But if you stick with it, learn from every pitch, and keep refining your approach, you'll get better. And eventually, you'll find the people who say "yes."

"Success is not the key to happiness. Happiness is the key to success. If you love what you are doing, you will be successful." - **Albert Schweitzer**

Chapter 23: Managing Rejection – When Your Pitch Lands with a Thud

The entrepreneurs who succeed aren't the ones who avoid rejection—they're the ones who know how to handle it, learn from it, and come back stronger. So let's talk about how to manage rejection when your pitch lands with a thud—and why this is some of the business bullshit you've got to deal with if you want to make it in this world.

You can have the perfect pitch, the best product, and a killer track record, and you'll still get shut down. Sometimes it's a polite "not right now," sometimes it's a brutal "this isn't for us," and sometimes it's just a blank stare while they scroll on their phone.

Rejection sucks. It feels personal—even when it's not. It'll make you question your idea, your approach, and maybe even yourself. But here's the thing: rejection isn't the end of the road. It's part of the job description.

Expect to Be Rejected

Here's the first rule of managing rejection: expect it. If you walk into every pitch thinking you're going to hit it out of the park, you're setting yourself up for disappointment.

But if you go in knowing there's a good chance you'll hear "no," you'll be ready to handle it—and ready to move on to the next step.

Rejection doesn't mean your idea is bad, your pitch was terrible, or you're not cut out for this. It just means that, for whatever reason, that particular opportunity didn't work out. And that's okay.

The Mindset Shift: Rejection isn't failure—it's feedback. Treat every "no" as a chance to learn, improve, and get closer to a "yes."

Ask Them Why

When someone rejects your pitch, don't just pack up and leave. Ask why. Nine times out of ten, the reason will fall into one of three categories:

A. Cost Is Too High

Let's face it—price is a sticking point for a lot of people. If they think your product or service is too expensive, it doesn't necessarily mean you're charging too much. It might just mean you haven't done a good enough job of showing them the value.

What to Do:

- Reframe the conversation around ROI (return on investment).

- Show them how your solution will save them money, time, or headaches in the long run.

- Remind them that quality work costs money—and cheap solutions usually end up costing more in the end.

B. Lack of Specifications

Sometimes, a prospect will say no because they don't think your product or service meets their specific needs. Maybe they need a feature you don't offer, or they think you don't understand their problem well enough.

What to Do:

- Ask detailed questions about what they're looking for.

- Highlight the flexibility of your solution. If you can tailor your offering to meet their needs, let them know.

- Be clear about what you *can* deliver—and why it's the best option for them.

C. Time Constraints

This one is common: they love your pitch, but they don't think you can deliver on their timeline. Maybe they're on a tight deadline, or they've already committed to another provider.

What to Do:

- Reassure them about your ability to meet deadlines. Share examples of how you've delivered on time in the past.

- If their timeline is truly impossible, be honest about it—but offer a solution. Maybe you can deliver part of the project now and the rest later, or maybe you can expedite the process for an additional cost.

Reiterate Your Strengths

When someone rejects your pitch, it's easy to feel like you've lost all leverage. But here's the thing: just because they said no doesn't mean they're not interested. Sometimes, they just need a little nudge to reconsider.

This is where you remind them why they should want to work with you. Reiterate your company's strengths and ask them directly if those are the qualities they're looking for.

Example:

- *"I understand that cost is a concern, but let me remind you of what we bring to the table: high-quality work, delivered on time, with a proven track record of success. Is that what you're looking for in a partner?"*

This does two things:

1. It refocuses the conversation on the value you provide.

2. It puts the ball back in their court. If they say yes, you've got an opportunity to address their objections and keep the conversation going.

4. Always Ask to Get Hired

Here's a hard truth: most people won't hire you unless you ask them to. Even after they've rejected your pitch, you should always ask for the opportunity to work with them.

Why? Because "no" doesn't always mean "never." Sometimes it just means "not right now" or "I'm not sure yet." By asking directly, you force them to either reconsider—or give you a concrete reason why they're not ready to move forward.

Example:

*   *"I'd love the opportunity to work with you. Is there anything holding you back from saying yes today?"*

*   *"If you're still on the fence, I'd be happy to address any concerns you have. What would it take for us to move forward?"*

The Bullshit You'll Face

Here's why managing rejection can feel like such a grind:

1. **It Feels Personal.** Even when the rejection has nothing to do with you, it's hard not to take it personally.

2. **You Don't Always Get Closure.** Some people will ghost you after saying no, leaving you wondering what went wrong.

3. **It's Exhausting.** Hearing "no" over and over again can wear you down, no matter how thick your skin is.

But here's the silver lining: every rejection brings you closer to a "yes." The more pitches you make, the more you learn, and the better you get at handling objections.

The Bottom Line

Rejection is part of the entrepreneurial journey. You can't avoid it, but you *can* learn to manage it. Expect it, embrace it, and use it as a tool to improve your pitch, refine your approach, and get better at selling your idea.

And above all, remember this: a "no" today doesn't mean "no" forever. Stay persistent, stay professional, and keep showing up. Because the only thing worse than rejection is giving up before you've even given yourself a chance.

"I have not failed. I've just found 10,000 ways that won't work." - **Thomas Edison**

Chapter 24: Filing Bankruptcy - The Best Move?

Bankruptcy. Just hearing the word feels like a gut punch, doesn't it? It's the boogeyman of the business world—the thing no one wants to talk about but every entrepreneur secretly fears. And for good reason. Filing for bankruptcy isn't just about admitting your business is in trouble—it's a nuclear option that can leave a mark on your financial reputation for decades.

But here's the thing: bankruptcy isn't always the end of the road. For some businesses, it's a way to hit the reset button and start fresh. For others, it's a devastating misstep that can haunt them for years. *Deciding whether to file or not is one of the toughest—and most bullshit-filled—choices an entrepreneur can face.*

So let's break this down. If you're staring down the barrel of a financial disaster, here's what you need to know before you even *think* about filing for bankruptcy.

1. Try Everything Possible to Avoid Bankruptcy

Let me make this crystal clear: bankruptcy should be your *very, very* last resort. I'm talking "the ship is on fire, the life rafts are full, and you're clinging to a piece of driftwood" kind of last resort.

Why? Because bankruptcy isn't just a quick fix. It's a financial scarlet letter that can follow you for decades. Sure, the lawyers and bankruptcy courts will tell you it's just a "seven-year blemish" on your credit report, but that's only part of the story. Banks, lenders, and even some business partners will see that bankruptcy filing and think, *This guy couldn't manage his money—why should we trust him now?*

If you've reached the point where you're considering bankruptcy, ask yourself: *Have I truly exhausted every other option?* Because trust me, there are options.

2. Creditors Don't Want You to File

Here's a little secret most people don't realize: your creditors *do not* want you to file for bankruptcy. Why? Because if you file, they're likely to get nothing—unless you've got significant assets they can seize.

Creditors aren't in the business of losing money. They'd much rather work out a deal with you than watch your debt vanish into a bankruptcy court filing. That's why negotiating with your creditors should always be your first move.

- Start the Conversation. Call your creditors and explain your situation. Be honest—tell them you're struggling but want to make things right.

- Propose a Plan. Offer to pay what you can, even if it's less than the full amount. Many creditors will accept reduced payments or extended timelines if it means getting something instead of nothing. Creditors will even consider 5-10 year payment plans.

- Leverage Their Fear of Bankruptcy. Let them know you're trying to avoid filing for bankruptcy, but it's on the table if they're unwilling to work with you. That's often enough to make them more flexible.

Pro Tip: You'd be surprised how many creditors are willing to negotiate if you approach them the right way. They might cut your debt in half, waive late fees, or set up a manageable payment plan. But you'll never know unless you ask.

3. Protect Your Credit Score

Here's another reason to avoid bankruptcy at all costs: it can absolutely wreck your credit score. And while it's true that a bankruptcy filing officially drops off your credit report after seven years, the damage can linger far longer than that.

Think about it: banks and lenders don't just look at your credit score—they look at your credit history. And seeing a bankruptcy on your record, even 10 or 15 years down the line, is enough to make them think twice about giving you a loan.

The Long-Term Impact:

- You might be denied loans or credit lines for years, even if your financial situation improves.

- If you do get approved for financing, you'll likely face sky-high interest rates.

- Your reputation as a business owner can take a hit, making it harder to attract investors or partners.

Bottom line: filing for bankruptcy isn't just a short-term solution. It's a long-term gamble that can cost you far more than you realize.

4. Negotiate First, Lawyer Up Later

If you've done everything you can to negotiate with your creditors and you're still drowning, it might be time to call in the pros. But here's the key: don't hire a bankruptcy attorney until you've done all the legwork yourself.

Why? Because lawyers are expensive—and they're not going to do the heavy lifting of negotiating with creditors for you. That's your job. Once you've talked to everyone and explored every option, then you bring in an attorney to handle the legal side of things.

What a Bankruptcy Attorney Will Do:

- Help you understand the different types of bankruptcy (personal vs. business, Chapter 7 vs. Chapter 11, etc.).

- Advise you on whether bankruptcy is truly necessary—or if there's another way to resolve your financial issues.

- Navigate the legal process and paperwork if you do decide to file.

Pro Tip: A good bankruptcy attorney isn't just there to file documents—they're there to help you avoid bankruptcy if possible. Make sure you hire someone who has your best interests in mind, not just their billable hours.

5. Decide: Personal or Business Bankruptcy?

If you've reached the point where bankruptcy seems unavoidable, the next question is: are you filing as an individual or as a business? And trust me, this decision matters—a lot.

Personal Bankruptcy

- This is usually the route if your business isn't incorporated or if you've personally guaranteed business debts.

- It means your personal assets (like your house, car, or savings) could be at risk.

- It's a more straightforward process, but the consequences for your personal credit can be severe.

Business Bankruptcy

- This is an option if your business is a separate legal entity (like an LLC or corporation).

- It allows you to liquidate the business's assets to pay off creditors without affecting your personal finances— assuming you haven't personally guaranteed any debts.

- It's more complex and expensive but can protect your personal credit and assets if done correctly.

Pro Tip: If you're not sure which type of bankruptcy to file, consult with an attorney or financial advisor who specializes in small business. They'll help you weigh the pros and cons based on your specific situation.

The Bullshit You'll Face

Let's not sugarcoat it—navigating bankruptcy is a a learning experience for sure. Here's some of the bullshit you're likely to encounter along the way:

1. **The Stigma.** Even though bankruptcy is more common than you think, it still carries a stigma. People will judge you, even if they don't know the full story.

2. **The Bureaucracy.** The paperwork, court filings, and legal hoops you'll have to jump through can feel overwhelming.

3. **The Emotional Toll.** Filing for bankruptcy isn't just a financial decision—it's an emotional one. It can feel like failure, even when it's not.

The Bottom Line

Bankruptcy isn't the end of the world—but it's not a decision to take lightly, either. Before you even consider filing, exhaust every other option. Negotiate with your creditors, cut costs wherever you can, and do everything in your power to keep your business afloat.

If bankruptcy does become your only option, approach it strategically. Hire the right professionals, protect your personal assets, and use it as an opportunity to start fresh—not as a crutch to avoid tough decisions. Your expertise and skillset can get another company back up and run without delays because by now, you know how to start up a new company.

Because at the end of the day, entrepreneurship isn't about avoiding failure, it's about learning how to bounce back, no matter what.

Elizabeth Warren *has described bankruptcy as "financial death and financial rebirth, while she noted that medical debts are a leading cause of bankruptcy."*

Chapter 25: Managing and Selecting the Best Independent Contractors

Here's the reality of entrepreneurship: no matter how talented or hardworking you are, you can't do it all. You're going to need help. And unless you're running a Fortune 500 company with a massive payroll budget, that help is going to come in the form of independent contractors.

Make no mistake about independent contractors are a critical part of any business. They fill the gaps that your full-time team can't cover, and they bring specialized skills you simply can't afford to hire in-house. Whether it's bookkeepers, CPAs, cleaners, tradespeople, or specialists, they're the lifeblood of your operations. But here's the catch: managing and selecting the *right* contractors is where the business bullshit starts to pile up.

A great independent contractor can make your life easier, elevate your reputation in the eyes of your customer, save you time, and boost your bottom line. A bad one? They can cost you money, ruin your reputation, and give you a headache the size of Texas. So let's talk about how to find the good ones, manage them effectively, and avoid the nonsense that comes with hiring the wrong people.

The Golden Rules of Selecting Contractors

The first step in managing contractors is picking the right ones. This is where a lot of entrepreneurs screw up—because they don't do their homework.

1. Check Their Credentials

This is non-negotiable. Always, *always* make sure your contractors are properly licensed, insured, and bonded.

- **Licensing:** This ensures they've met the minimum standards of their trade or profession. If something goes wrong, you have leverage—you can file a complaint against their license, and trust me, they'll take that seriously.

- **Liability Insurance:** If they damage your property, injure someone, or screw up the job, their insurance should cover it—not you or your customer.

- **Worker's Compensation:** If they get injured on the job and don't have workers' comp, guess who they're coming after? You. Protect yourself by making sure they're covered.

2. Get References or Referrals

The best way to find great contractors is to ask the people you trust. Your best contractors, suppliers, or colleagues are often your best sources for referrals. If someone's already done great work for people you know, chances are they'll do great work for you too.

3. Start Small

Before you trust a contractor with a big, high-stakes project, test them out on something smaller. This gives you a chance to see how they work, how reliable they are, and whether they're a good fit for your business.

4. Weed Out the Red Flags

Trust your gut. If a contractor seems disorganized, unprofessional, or makes excuses before they've even started, walk away. It's better to delay a project than to hire someone who's going to cause problems down the line.

How to Manage Contractors Without Losing Your Mind

Hiring the right contractors is only half the battle. Managing them effectively is where the real work begins.

1. Pay Them on Time

This is the number one rule for keeping good contractors happy: pay them on time, every time. I recommend paying contractors every Friday. It shows respect for their work and keeps them motivated to prioritize your projects.

2. Treat Them with Respect

Contractors aren't your employees—they're your partners. Treat them with gratitude and professionalism. Compliment their work, thank them for their efforts, and show them you value their contributions.

I highly recommend not giving them all of your work—only 2-3 jobs at a time. Otherwise, if you give them 5-10 jobs, now they will have leverage on you! Start out slow and cautiously.

Contractors aren't your employees—they're your partners. Treat them with gratitude and professionalism. Compliment their work, thank them for their efforts, and show them you value their contributions.

Pro Tip: If you really want to make an impression, compliment them *in front of your customers*. It builds goodwill and makes them more likely to go above and beyond for you.

3. Handle Problems Wisely

Even the best contractors will screw up from time to time. When that happens, you need to handle it carefully.

- Leverage Their License: If a contractor refuses to fix they faulty work remind them that you can file a complaint against their license. You'd be surprised how quickly they'll fix the problem to avoid that. The best contractors will not hesitate to go back immediately and fix their work because they value all the work you give them during the year.

- Know When to Cut Your Losses: Sometimes, it's better to pay a bad contractor to go away. Have them sign a lien release, pay them off, and never hire them again. It's not worth the embarrassment of them going directly to your customer for payment.

The Three Types of Contractors

Not all contractors are created equal. Over the years, I've found that they generally fall into three categories:

1. The Good

- Traits: Decent work, but not perfect. They're often late to meetings (30 minutes to an hour isn't uncommon).

- Best Use: Put these contractors on low-income or simple projects where their quality and speed won't hurt your reputation.

2. The Better

- Traits: Higher-quality work, more punctual, and generally reliable. They're great for straightforward projects that don't require a lot of customer interaction or complex problem-solving.

- Best Use: Assign them to medium-sized projects where you need consistency but don't require perfection.

3. The Best

- Traits: Top-notch work, excellent communication, and reliability you can count on. These are the ones who make you look good in front of your customers.

- Best Use: Save these contractors for high-stakes projects where quality and timeliness are critical.

- You pay them more, but they can be worth every penny. If you feel the company can not afford their rates, keep looking as other companies would love to have all the work you will give them.

Pro Tip: Your best contractors are your most valuable asset. Treat them like gold, and they'll stick with you for years.

The Bullshit You'll Face

Working with independent contractors isn't all sunshine and rainbows. Here's some of the nonsense you'll have to deal with:

1. **Missed Deadlines:** Even the good ones can drop the ball sometimes. Build extra time into your timeline to account for this.

2. **Inconsistent Quality:** Not every contractor will meet your standards. Be clear about your expectations upfront and hold them accountable.

3. **Communication Issues:** Some contractors are great at their trade but terrible at responding to emails or calls. Set clear communication protocols from the start.

The Bottom Line

When you find contractors who are reliable, skilled, and easy to work with, hold onto them. Pay them on time, show your appreciation, and keep them happy. Because at the end of the day, great contractors aren't just helping you get the job done—they're helping you build your business.

"I think it is possible for ordinary people to choose to be extraordinary." **- Elon Musk**

Chapter 26: Owning and Managing the Company Website

Let's talk about websites. That magical slice of the internet where your business lives, your customers come to check you out, and you silently pray no one notices the typos you missed on your "About Us" page.

When I first started my business, the idea of building a website felt both thrilling and terrifying. On one hand, it was proof that my business was real—a digital storefront for the world to see. On the other hand, I had no clue what I was doing.

I hired a professional web developer and the price was a reasonable and affordable $7,500, but then I saw the amount of money I had to pay monthly for them to make small changes was astronomical. Let's just say it was slightly above my "new business budget."

Building and Managing a Website Without Losing Your Mind

Running a website doesn't have to be overwhelming. Here are the lessons I've learned along the way:

1. Start with the Basics

Before you dive into website builders and templates, take a step back and think about what you actually need. Ask yourself:

- What's the purpose of my website?

- Who's my audience?

- What information do I need to include?

When I built my first website, I tried to put *everything* on it—a blog, a photo gallery, a page about my cat. The result? A cluttered mess.

Now, I focus on the essentials:

- A clear homepage that explains what I do.

- An "About" page to tell my story.

- A "Services" or "Products" page.

- A contact page so people can reach me.

Start simple. You can always expand later.

2. Choose the Right Platform

There are countless website platforms out there, so it's easy to get overwhelmed. My advice? Pick one that matches your needs and skill level.

Here are a few popular options:

- Wix: Great for beginners who want a simple drag-and-drop builder.

- Squarespace: Sleek and stylish, perfect for creative businesses.

- WordPress: More complex but highly customizable if you want full control.

- Shopify: The go-to platform for e-commerce businesses.

I went with WordPress for the customization options, but I'll admit—it came with a learning curve. If you're not a fan of tinkering, a simpler platform might be a better fit.

3. Keep It User-Friendly

Your website isn't just for you—it's for your customers. Make sure it's easy to navigate, loads quickly, and works on both desktop and mobile devices.

One of my early mistakes was cramming my homepage with too much information. I thought I was being thorough, but I was really just confusing people. Now, I follow the "less is more" rule:

- Clean design.

- Clear navigation.

- A focus on the most important content.

4. Learn the Basics of SEO

Search Engine Optimization (SEO) might sound intimidating, but it's not as complicated as you think. At its core, SEO is about making your website easy for search engines (and people) to find.

Here's what worked for me:

- Use keywords your audience is searching for.

- Write clear, descriptive headlines.

- Add meta descriptions to your pages.

When I started paying attention to SEO, my website traffic improved almost immediately.

5. Make It Easy to Update

Your website isn't a "set it and forget it" project. You'll need to update it regularly, so choose a platform that makes this easy.

I learned this the hard way when I tried to update my first website and accidentally deleted my entire "About" page. (Cue panic and a lot of swearing.) Now, I always back up my site before making changes. Trust me, it's worth the effort.

Maintaining Your Website Without Losing Your Sanity

Once your website is live, the real work begins: keeping it fresh and functional. Here's how I manage mine without turning it into a full-time job:

1. Set a Maintenance Schedule

I check in on my website once a week. It doesn't take long—usually 20-30 minutes—but it keeps things running smoothly.

2. Add Fresh Content

Search engines love fresh content, and so do visitors. Whether it's a blog post, a new product, or updated testimonials, adding something new every month keeps your site relevant.

3. Monitor Analytics

Most website platforms come with built-in analytics tools. Use them! They'll show you how visitors are interacting with your site and where you can improve.

For example, I once noticed that my contact page was getting a ton of traffic but almost no submissions. Turns out, my contact form was broken. Oops.

The Bottom Line

Managing your website doesn't have to be overwhelming. Start simple, choose tools that work for you, and embrace the learning process. Sure, you'll make mistakes along the way (we all do), but that's part of the journey.

Your website is more than just an online presence—it's a reflection of your business, your brand, and your hard work. So take the time to make it something you're proud of. And if all else fails, remember: there's always tech support.

"Innovation distinguishes between a leader and a follower." -**Steve Jobs**

Chapter 27: Website Marketing

Here's the thing no one tells you about building a website: just because you build it doesn't mean people will magically show up. When I first launched my company's site, I thought, *Great, now I'm online! Customers will start pouring in any day now!* Spoiler alert: they didn't.

A website is like a storefront on a deserted street unless you market it. People won't stumble on your site by accident. You've got to show them the way—whether it's through Google, social media, or paid ads.

The good news? Marketing your website isn't rocket science. The bad news? It takes effort, trial and error, and a willingness to learn a whole new bag of tricks. Let me walk you through what I've learned about driving traffic, boosting visibility, and turning your website into a customer magnet.

The Harsh Truth About Website Traffic

Here's the harsh truth: the internet is crowded. Your website is one of billions. If you want people to find it, you have to make some noise. And by "noise," I mean employing smart marketing strategies that cut through the clutter and get your site in front of the right people.

When I first started marketing my website, I had no idea where to begin. Should I focus on SEO? Should I pay for ads? Should I just write some blog posts and hope someone stumbles across them? The answer, I learned, is a mix of all the above. Let's break it down.

Google Pay-Per-Click Ads (PPC)

Let's talk about Google Ads, also known as pay-per-click (PPC) advertising. I'll be honest: the idea of paying for website traffic felt like cheating at first. But when I realized how hard it was to get organic traffic, I decided to give it a shot.

Here's how PPC works:

- You create an ad that appears at the top of Google search results when someone searches for specific keywords.

- You only pay when someone clicks on your ad.

Sounds simple, right? Well, yes and no. Here's what I've learned about running PPC campaigns:

1. Start Small

When I ran my first Google Ads campaign, I made the mistake of targeting way too many keywords and blowing through my budget in no time. Now, I start small—focusing on a handful of highly relevant keywords and testing what works before scaling up.

2. Focus on High-Intent Keywords

Not all clicks are created equal. If someone's searching "What is [my industry]?" They might just be looking for information. But if they're searching "Buy [product/service] near me," they're ready to pull the trigger. Focus your ads on high-intent keywords that attract people who are ready to take action.

3. Set a Budget

PPC can get expensive fast if you're not careful. Set a daily or monthly budget and stick to it. I learned this the hard way when I forgot to cap my spending and racked up a bill that made my jaw drop.

4. Track Your Results

Google Ads comes with analytics tools that show you which keywords and ads are driving traffic—and which ones aren't. Use this data to optimize your campaigns and get the best bang for your buck.

SEO: The Long Game

If PPC is the fast track to website traffic, Search Engine Optimization (SEO) is the long game. SEO is all about making your website show up in organic (non-paid) search results, and while it takes time to see results, it's one of the most cost-effective ways to drive traffic.

When I first heard about SEO, it sounded like a foreign language. Keywords? Meta descriptions? Backlinks? I didn't know where to start. But once I got the hang of it, I realized it wasn't as scary as I thought. Here's what worked for me:

1. Choose the Right Keywords

Keywords are the foundation of SEO. These are the words and phrases people type into Google when they're looking for something. For example, if you run a bakery, your keywords might include "best cupcakes near me" or "custom wedding cakes."

I use tools like Google Keyword Planner and Ubersuggest to find keywords with high search volume and low competition. The goal is to target terms that people are searching for but aren't overly saturated.

2. Optimize Your Pages

Once you've identified your keywords, sprinkle them throughout your website—in headlines, page titles, meta descriptions, and body text. But don't overdo it. Google penalizes sites that "keyword stuff," so make sure your content reads naturally.

3. Create High-Quality Content

One of the best ways to improve your SEO is by creating valuable, engaging content that answers your audience's questions. Blog posts, guides, and FAQs are all great options.

When I started blogging regularly, I noticed a steady increase in organic traffic. The key is to write for your audience, not just for search engines. If people find your content helpful, Google will too.

4. Build Backlinks

Backlinks—links from other websites to yours—are like votes of confidence in the eyes of Google. The more high-quality backlinks you have, the higher your site will rank.

I've built backlinks by networking with other business owners, guest posting on industry blogs, and getting featured in local news stories. It takes effort, but the payoff is worth it.

Keywords: The Secret Sauce

Whether you're running PPC campaigns or optimizing for SEO, keywords are the secret sauce that ties everything together. Here are a few tips for making the most of them:

1. Think Like Your Customer

Put yourself in your customer's shoes. What would they type into Google if they were looking for your product or service? Use this as a starting point for your keyword research.

2. Use Long-Tail Keywords

Long-tail keywords are longer, more specific phrases like "affordable web design for small businesses" instead of just "web design." They're less competitive and often attract more qualified leads.

3. Keep Testing

Keywords aren't a one-and-done deal. Trends change, and so do search habits. Regularly review your keyword strategy and adjust as needed.

<u>Lessons Learned the Hard Way</u>

Like most things in business, marketing my website has come with its fair share of mistakes and "oops" moments. Here are a few lessons I've learned:

1. **Don't Expect Overnight Results**

   SEO takes time. PPC requires fine-tuning. If you're not seeing immediate results, don't panic—just keep experimenting and improving.

2. **Avoid the "Set It and Forget It" Trap**

   Whether it's an ad campaign or an SEO strategy, nothing runs itself. Regular maintenance and updates are key to staying ahead.

3. **Focus on Quality Over Quantity**

When I first started blogging, I cranked out as many posts as possible. But they weren't great, and they didn't attract much traffic. Now, I focus on creating fewer, higher-quality pieces that offer real value.

The Takeaway

Marketing your website isn't optional. It's the engine that drives traffic, attracts customers, and keeps your business growing. Whether you're investing in Google Ads, mastering SEO, or fine-tuning your keyword strategy, the key is to stay consistent, stay curious, and keep learning.

Because at the end of the day, your website is more than just a digital storefront, it's the heart of your online presence. And if you take the time to market it right, it can become one of your business's most powerful tools.

"Quality is remembered long after price is forgotten." - **Aldo Gucci**

Chapter 28: Deconstructing Business Jargon and Buzzwords

Let's talk about business jargon and buzzwords—the verbal junk food of the professional world. You've heard them. You've probably even used them. "Let's circle back." "We need to leverage our synergies." "This project needs more bandwidth."

At first, this language might seem like the secret handshake of the professional world. You hear it, and you think, *This is how smart people talk. This is how you get taken seriously.* But after a while, you realize something—most of it is complete and utter bullshit.

Buzzwords don't solve problems. They don't close deals. And they definitely don't make you a better entrepreneur. What they do is waste time, confuse people, and make you sound like you're trying too hard to impress someone. The truth is, the more buzzwords you use, the less you actually say.

But here's the kicker: as much as I hate jargon, you're going to encounter it everywhere in business. Meetings, emails, pitches—it's like a virus that's infected every corner of the professional world. And like it or not, you're going to have to deal with it.

The Anatomy of Business Bullshit

Business jargon is what happens when people try to sound smarter than they actually are. It's a mix of overcomplicated phrases, vague buzzwords, and corporate slang that's designed to make simple ideas sound sophisticated.

Let me translate a few classics for you:

- **"Let's circle back."** Translation: I have no idea what to say right now, so let's pretend we'll talk about this later.

- **"We need to leverage our synergies."** Translation: I don't know how to collaborate effectively, so I'm going to throw some fancy words at the problem.
- **"Let's take this offline."** Translation: I don't want to deal with this in front of everyone, so let's argue about it in private.
- **"We're thinking outside the box."** Translation: We're doing the same thing everyone else is doing, but we're going to act like it's groundbreaking.
- **"Low-hanging fruit."** Translation: The easiest stuff to do, which we'll overcomplicate anyway.

It's not just the phrases—it's the way they're used. These words are often deployed to avoid accountability, mask a lack of real ideas, or just fill dead air in a meeting. And the worst part? People eat it up.

Why Jargon Is Everywhere

You might wonder, *Why is this nonsense so common if it's so useless?* Here's what I've figured out:

1. **It's a Crutch for Insecurity.**

   A lot of people, especially in business, are terrified of looking stupid. Instead of admitting they don't know something, they hide behind big words and vague phrases. It's easier to say you're "leveraging synergies" than to admit you don't have a real plan.

2. **It Creates the Illusion of Expertise.**

   Buzzwords make people sound like they know what they're talking about—even when they don't. If you can throw enough jargon into a pitch or a meeting, you might convince people you're smarter than you actually are. (Spoiler: This strategy doesn't hold up over time.)

3. **It's Contagious.**

   Once jargon enters a workplace, it spreads like wildfire. If your boss says "circle back" in every meeting, you'll start saying it too—whether you like it or not.

4. **It's a Status Symbol.**

   In some industries, jargon is basically a badge of honor. If you're not throwing around terms like "scalability" and "market disruption," people might assume you don't belong.

How to Cut Through the Noise

Dealing with jargon is one of those business challenges you can't avoid. But you don't have to let it take over your communication. Here's how I've learned to handle it.

1. Say What You Actually Mean

This seems obvious, but it's harder than it sounds. It takes effort to strip away the fluff and get to the point. Instead of saying, "We need to leverage our core competencies," just say, "Let's focus on what we do best."

Clear, simple language is always more effective than buzzwords. People will appreciate your honesty, and they'll actually understand what you're saying.

2. Call Out the Bullshit

When someone starts spewing jargon, don't be afraid to ask questions. "What do you mean by that?" or "Can you explain that in plain English?" forces people to clarify their ideas. If they can't, you've just exposed the fluff for what it is.

3. Use Jargon Strategically

Here's the thing: sometimes you have to play the game. If you're pitching to a client who lives and breathes buzzwords, you might need to throw in a few "disruptive innovations" or "value propositions" to speak their language. But use this sparingly, and only when it serves a purpose.

4. Practice Jargon Immunity

Don't let jargon infect your thinking. Just because everyone else is saying something doesn't mean it's valuable. Train yourself to question buzzwords and focus on substance over style.

The Bottom Line on Jargon

Jargon and buzzwords are some of the most frustrating parts of the business world. They waste time, confuse people, and turn simple ideas into convoluted nonsense.

But here's the good news: you don't have to buy into it. The best entrepreneurs—the ones who actually get things done—aren't the ones throwing around the most buzzwords. They're the ones who know how to communicate clearly, think critically, and cut through the noise.

So the next time someone tells you to "circle back" or "leverage your synergies," don't roll your eyes too hard. Decode the message, respond with clarity, and keep your bullshit radar on high alert.

Because in a world full of buzzwords, the smartest people are the ones who know when to call it what it really is—bullshit.

"The best preparation for tomorrow is doing your best today." – **H. Jackson Brown, Jr.**

Chapter 29: Crazy, Insane Customers

Let's get one thing straight—if you're running a business, you *will* encounter crazy, insane customers. It's not a matter of "if," but "when." No matter how good your service is, no matter how hard you work to make things right, some people are just impossible to please. It's one of those unavoidable truths of entrepreneurship— and it's some of the most frustrating business bullshit you'll ever have to deal with.

My company performs over 50 large-scale projects a year, and year after year, I find our staff dealing with 2–3 customers who make me question my sanity. I'm talking about the ones who complain about everything, refuse to acknowledge your efforts, and never seem satisfied, no matter what you do.

And here's the worst part—those 2–3 customers? They're the ones I remember at the end of the year. Not the 47 or 48 happy, wonderful customers who loved our work and appreciated our efforts. Nope. It's the crazies who stick in my mind, eating up my energy and leaving me wondering, *What the hell could I have done differently?*

Why the Crazy Customers Stick with Us

So why do these nightmare customers have such a grip on us? Why do we let them overshadow all the positive feedback from the rest of our clients?

It's simple: because as business owners, we care. I care deeply about my company's reputation, about my team's hard work, and about making sure every customer leaves satisfied. That's not just lip service—it's a core part of who I am as a business owner.

I believe in this philosophy: you can be a bad company, an average company, a good company, an excellent company—or an *elite* company. My goal, day in and day out, is to be elite. I talk about this with my staff at our weekly meetings because this mentality drives everything we do.

And when you're striving to be elite, those 2–3 customers who refuse to be happy feel like a personal failure. Even when you know deep down that you did everything you could, their dissatisfaction can feel like a black mark on your year.

How to Handle Crazy Customers Without Losing Your Sanity

Over the years, I've developed some strategies for dealing with these kinds of customers. They're not foolproof—nothing is when you're dealing with unreasonable people—but they've helped me keep my sanity and protect my business's reputation.

1. Treat Every Customer with Respect—Even the Difficult Ones

Let me be clear: just because a customer is unreasonable doesn't mean you get to be unprofessional. Your job is to treat every customer with respect and handle every situation as professionally as possible. ***The easiest way to do this is to take the emotion out of the equation and stick to the business issue at hand.... how to WE all solve this moving forward amicably.***

Why? Because even if you can't make them happy, other people are watching. Your employees, your other customers, and anyone else who hears about the situation will judge your business based on how you handle it.

That said, respect is a two-way street. If a customer is rude, insulting, or outright dishonest, I won't hesitate to call them out. I'll tell them, *"This is not the type of relationship I strive for with my customers. I want us both to be happy and enjoy the process."*

2. Go the Extra Mile—But Set Your Limits

When a project goes sideways, my first instinct is always to fix it. I'll spend extra time, throw more money at the problem, and even offer credit on the final invoice if that's what it takes to make things right. Why? Because that's what an elite company does.

But here's the hard truth: some customers don't want to be happy. No matter how much you bend over backward, they'll find something to complain about. When you realize you're dealing with one of *those* customers, you need to set clear limits.

- **Fix the Problem, Not the Person:** Focus on resolving the issue at hand, not on trying to win the customer's approval.

- **Know When to Walk Away:** If a customer is making unreasonable demands or refuses to work with you in good faith, it may be time to cut your losses. However, I feel strongly to never abandon a project until complete or I would get fired.

3. Don't Let Them Embarrass You

One of the biggest risks with crazy customers is that they'll take their grievances directly to your other customers—or worse, to the public. This is a nightmare scenario for any business owner, and it's why you need to handle disputes carefully.

If you've decided to pay off a difficult customer and cut ties, make sure everything is documented and legally binding. A signed lien release or settlement agreement can prevent them from coming after your customers—later on.

And if they do try to stir up trouble? Stay calm, stay professional, and let your track record of great work speak for itself.

4. Focus on Your Great Customers

Here's the thing about crazy customers: they're loud. They demand your attention, even when they don't deserve it. But they're not the majority.

Most of your customers are good, reasonable people who appreciate your work and value your efforts. Don't let the crazy ones overshadow the positive relationships you've built.

- Celebrate your wins.

- Thank your loyal customers.

- Focus on the 47 or 48 happy clients who make your work worthwhile.

At the end of the day, those are the people who matter—not the 2–3 customers who can't be pleased.

The Bullshit You'll Face

No matter how hard you try, you'll never completely avoid crazy customers. They're part of the package when you're running a business. Here's some of the nonsense you'll have to deal with:

1. **Unreasonable Demands:** They'll ask for things that are impossible, impractical, or way outside the scope of your agreement.

2. **Personal Attacks:** Some customers will cross the line, making rude or insulting comments about you, your team, or your business.

3. **Public Complaints:** If they're unhappy, they might air their grievances on social media, review sites, or even directly to your other customers.

The Bottom Line

Crazy, insane customers are a fact of life in business. You can't avoid them, but you can manage them—and you can decide how much power you're willing to give them over your time, energy, and sanity.

Remember: your job is to aim for excellence, not perfection. Treat every customer with respect, do your best to make things right, and focus on the clients who truly value your work.

Because at the end of the day, it's not the crazy customers who define your business—it's how you handle them that sets you apart as a bad, average, good, excellent, or elite company.

"Your most unhappy customers are your greatest source of learning." - ***Bill Gates***

Chapter 30: The Insurance Hustle

Let me tell you something about commercial insurance companies: they're not in the business of protecting you. They're in the business of protecting *themselves*. If you think having insurance means you're covered when disaster strikes, think again. This is one of those business realities they don't teach you in school. It's also one of the most frustrating and expensive types of business bullshit you're going to deal with as an entrepreneur.

Here's the thing about insurance companies. They're happy to take your premiums every year—quietly, without a peep. But the moment you actually need them? That's when the real fun begins. Let me paint you a picture. Imagine you've been paying your premiums for 30 years. You've never filed a claim, not once. Then, one day, your business floods, or your roof collapses, or there's a fire. You think, "No problem, I've got insurance." You file the claim, and sure enough, they cut you a check.

And then they raise your rates.

Yep, you heard that right. You're suddenly a "high-risk" customer because *you used the service you've been paying for decades to have.* It doesn't matter that this was your first claim in 30 years. It doesn't matter that you've been a loyal customer. They'll jack up your rates without batting an eye, as if you caused the flood or started the fire yourself. In some cases, they'll even drop you altogether. You're left scrambling to find new coverage—at an even higher premium—because now, you've got a claim history.

But it gets worse. Let's talk about the some of the homeowners in Los Angeles who recently lost everything in the fires. You'd think their insurance companies would step up, right? After all, that's the whole point of insurance. Wrong. Some of these homeowners were informed that their insurance policies were in their personal names, but their homes were held in family trusts. And guess what? That technicality gave the insurance companies a free pass to deny their claims.

Think about that for a second. These people lost their homes, and instead of getting the help they desperately needed, they were handed a legal loophole. It's not just cruel, it's calculated. These companies have teams of lawyers whose sole job is to find reasons *not* to pay you. And unless you have someone in your corner who knows how to navigate this nonsense, you're going to get steamrolled.

This is why having a reputable, knowledgeable insurance agent is non-negotiable. I'm not talking about the guy who sends you a birthday card every year and calls it service. I'm talking about someone who understands the fine print, who will fight for you, and who actually appreciates your business. You need someone who will go the extra yard to make sure your policies are airtight— because if they're not, you're the one who will pay for them.

Here are some key *red flags* to watch out for when choosing an insurance agent. Spotting these early can save you from unnecessary headaches—or worse, financial disaster—down the line:

1. Pushes the Cheapest Policy Without Explaining Coverage

- If an agent is overly focused on selling you the cheapest policy without discussing what it actually covers (or doesn't cover), that's a problem. Cheap often means incomplete, which can leave you exposed when you need the coverage most.

2. Dodges Your Questions

- A knowledgeable agent should be able to explain your policy options clearly and answer your questions without hesitation. If they're vague, dismissive, or constantly redirect conversations, they might not fully understand the products themselves—or worse, they're hiding something.

3. No Interest in Your Specific Needs

- A good agent will take the time to understand your business, assets, and risks. If they're not asking detailed questions about your operations, property ownership, or unique circumstances, they're likely selling generic policies that may not fit your situation.

4. No Track Record or References

- Experience matters. If the agent can't provide references, testimonials, or examples of how they've helped other clients in similar situations, you're taking a gamble. Look for someone with a solid reputation and proven expertise.

5. Overly Aggressive Sales Tactics

- Beware of agents who pressure you into making a decision immediately or who use scare tactics to close the deal. Insurance is important, but you should have the time to evaluate your options and feel confident about your choice.

6. Failure to Discuss Exclusions or Loopholes

- Every policy has exclusions—things it won't cover. If an agent glosses over this or avoids discussing the fine print, you could be blindsided later. A trustworthy agent will make sure you understand what's *not* covered just as much as what is.

7. No Regular Follow-Up or Reviews

- A good insurance agent doesn't disappear after they sell you a policy. If they're not offering to review your coverage annually or keeping you informed about changes in laws, regulations, or your industry, they might not have your best interests at heart.

8. Unwilling to Customize Policies

- If the agent insists on "one-size-fits-all" solutions or refuses to explore tailored options, it's a red flag. Your business and personal circumstances are unique, and your insurance should reflect that.

9. Lack of Licensing or Qualifications

- Always verify that the agent is licensed in your state and has the proper credentials to sell insurance. If they can't provide proof, walk away.

10. Negative Online Reviews or Complaints

Check online reviews, Better Business Bureau ratings, or state insurance department complaint records. A pattern of unresolved complaints or poor reviews is a major warning sign.

11. Overpromising or Guaranteeing Payouts

No agent can guarantee a claim will be paid—it's up to the insurance company and the terms of the policy. If they're making promises that sound too good to be true, they're probably just looking to close the deal.

12. Doesn't Offer Multiple Options

A quality agent will present you with several quotes or policy options from different carriers to ensure you're getting the best value. If they're only pushing one carrier or product, they might be more loyal to the insurer than to you.

13. Unclear About Who They Represent

Some agents work for a specific insurance company (captive agents), while others are independent and can shop around. If they're not upfront about who they represent, you won't know if they're offering you the best deal or just what their employer sells.

14. Fails to Address Business Entity Issues

As seen in the Los Angeles example, small details—like whether your home or business is owned personally or by a trust—can make or break your coverage. If the agent doesn't ask about or address these complexities, they're not doing their due diligence.

15. Difficult to Reach

If the agent is slow to respond during the sales process, imagine how hard it will be to reach them when you have a claim. Prompt communication is essential in a good insurance agent.

When you're running a business, insurance isn't optional. But don't make the mistake of thinking the insurance company is your partner. They're not. They're just another vendor, and like any vendor, they're looking out for themselves. The sooner you understand that the better off you'll be.

So, what's the takeaway here? Invest in a great insurance agent. Someone who will ask the right questions and make sure your policies actually cover what you think they cover. Someone who will call out bullshit before it becomes your problem. Because trust me, when it comes to insurance, the bullshit is baked in.

Chapter 31: Don't Die at the Hands of a Credit Card Company

Picture this: business is going well, maybe even thriving. You've got momentum, clients are happy, and you're ready to expand—bigger office, more inventory, or maybe a new product line. So, like any savvy entrepreneur, you decide to increase your credit line to fund the next step. You call up the credit card company, feeling confident. They've been sending you offers for years, right? This should be easy.

But instead of an approval letter, you get a notice telling you that you're dead. That's right, dead. According to their system, you've ceased to exist. Not only are you blindsided, but also now your accounts are frozen, your credit score tanks, and your business grinds to a halt.

Sounds like a bad joke, doesn't it? Except it's not funny, and it's more common than you think. Some lazy data entry clerks hit the wrong key, and suddenly you're fighting to prove you're alive. Meanwhile, the credit card company doesn't care. To them, you're just a number, and they're not in the business of fixing mistakes quickly.

Why Credit Cards Are Both a Tool and a Trap

Let me be clear: credit cards can be a great tool for entrepreneurs. They give you flexibility, points for travel and purchases, and cash back that can offset business expenses. But here's the catch— they're also a double-edged sword.

If you don't watch every statement, every transaction, and every interaction with the credit card company like a hawk, you're setting yourself up for disaster. And trust me, these companies are not your friends. They're not in the business of helping you succeed; they're in the business of making money off your mistakes.

The 30% Rule: Keep Your Credit in Check

One of the biggest traps entrepreneurs fall into is maxing out their credit cards or carrying a balance month after month. Here's the truth: using more than 30% of your available credit can crush your credit score, even if you're making payments on time.

You've got to think of your credit limit as a tool, not free money. Keep your charges under 30% of your limit each month. Better yet, pay off your balance in full. Not just to avoid interest (which is a no-brainer) but to keep your credit score strong. A strong credit score can mean the difference between getting that business loan you desperately need or being stuck in a cash-flow nightmare.

The Bullshit Behind the Scenes

Let's talk about the real problem: bullshit behind the scenes. Credit card companies have complex systems, faceless customer service reps, and layers of bureaucracy. They don't care about your business, your dreams, or the fact that one mistake on their end can ruin everything you've built.

Take my friend, for example. She was running a successful company, had excellent credit, and was ready to expand. Then came the letter saying she was dead. Her accounts were frozen, her credit score dropped over 400 points, and she's spent 20+ years untangling the mess. In the meantime, she lost customers, opportunities, and sleep.

How did it happen? Some idiot in a cubicle made a typo. That's it. And no one at the credit card company took responsibility. She has to fight tooth and nail to fix their mistake, while her business continues to suffer.

How to Protect Yourself from the Bullshit

Here's the bottom line: don't trust anyone to have your back when it comes to your finances.

1. **I check transactions EVERY DAY. Check Your Statements Religiously.**

   I don't care how busy you are—make time to review every line item on your credit card statement. Fraud happens, mistakes happen, and interest charges sneak in when you least expect it.

2. **Monitor Your Credit Score**

   Use tools like Credit Karma or Experian to track your score monthly. If something looks off, investigate immediately.

3. **Keep Your Balance Low**

   Remember the 30% rule. Better yet, pay off your balance in full every month. If you can't, you're living beyond your means, and it's only a matter of time before it catches up with you.

4. **Document Everything**

   Every call, every email, every interaction with your credit card company—document it. If something goes wrong, you'll want a paper trail to back you up.

5. **Have a Backup Plan**

Don't rely on one credit card or one line of credit. Diversify your options so one mistake won't take you down.

The Takeaway

Credit cards are a necessary evil in business. They can provide flexibility and rewards, but they can also destroy you if you're not careful. The bullshit entrepreneurs have to deal with when it comes to credit card companies is real, and it's not going away.

The key is to stay vigilant. Never assume someone else is handling things correctly—whether it's a data entry clerk, a customer service rep, or even your own accountant. Double-check everything, stay within your limits, and keep control of your financial destiny.

"If I had to run a company on three measures, those measures would be customer satisfaction, employee satisfaction, and cash flow," **says Jack Welch, former CEO of General Electric**

Chapter 32: Business Phones - A Tale of Rings, Texts, and Bullshit

Let me tell you something about business phones: they're one of those decisions that seems small on the surface but can snowball into a full-on pain in the ass if you don't get it right. It's not just about picking a phone system or handing out cell phones to your team, it's about navigating the endless bullshit that comes with it. But hey, that's entrepreneurship for you.

Here's the deal. If you're running a business, communication is the lifeblood of your operation. Calls, texts, voicemail all has to flow seamlessly. But what no one tells you is how much of a headache this seemingly simple decision can turn into.

First, let's talk about the options. You've got two main routes:

1. **A business phone system** (you know, the classic desk phones that make your office look like a legit operation).

2. **Cell phones for everyone** (because who doesn't love being reachable 24/7?).

Now, here's where the bullshit starts. You're going to have to weigh the pros and cons of each, all while juggling the needs of your business, your team, and your wallet.

The Case for Cell Phones

If your business thrives on text messaging—think sales teams, customer service, or anything that requires constant back-and-forth—cell phones are a no-brainer. Texting is quick, direct, and honestly, it's how people communicate these days. Plus, giving every employee a company cell phone means they're always connected, whether they're in the office, on the road, or working from home.

The downside? Cell phones can blur the line between work and personal life. Suddenly, your team is getting work texts at 10 PM on a Saturday. And let's not forget the cost. Buying and maintaining cell phones for every employee isn't cheap. Plus, you've got to trust your team not to abuse their company phone for personal use. Spoiler alert: someone will.

The Case for a Phone System

If you've got a bigger team—10 employees or more—a dedicated phone system starts to make sense. These systems can handle multiple lines, offer call recording, and even let you set up extensions so customers can reach the right person without playing phone tag.

The biggest advantage? Control. With a phone system, you've got a clear record of every call made and received. It's professional, organized, and keeps the personal lives of your employees out of the equation.

But here's the catch: phone systems aren't cheap either. You'll be paying for the hardware, installation, and ongoing maintenance. And if your team works remotely or travels often, those desk phones suddenly become useless paperweights.

The Bullshit You'll Deal With

No matter which routes you choose, there's going to be bullshit. With cell phones, it's constant connectivity and potential for misuse. With phone systems, it's the cost and the rigidity. Either way, you'll need to lay down some ground rules to make sure things run smoothly.

For cell phones, set clear boundaries. Let your employees know when it's okay to shut off their work phones and enjoy their personal time. For phone systems, invest in a setup that's flexible enough to adapt to your team's needs, like systems that integrate with mobile apps for remote workers.

The Bottom Line

Here's my advice: think about what your business needs before you make a decision. If you're a small team that relies heavily on texting, go with cell phones. If you're running a larger operation with a lot of incoming calls, the phone system is probably the better bet. Either way, make sure you've got a system that tracks calls so you can hold everyone accountable. This is just one of the many decisions you'll have to make as an entrepreneur.

Chapter 33: Pros and Cons of Sleepless Nights

Every entrepreneur has sleepless nights. If you think you're going to build a business without losing sleep, you're either delusional or not trying hard enough. The truth is, some nights you'll find yourself lying there in bed, staring at the ceiling, your mind racing like a freight train you can't stop. You're thinking about the proposal you need to get to the potential customer, deadlines, missed opportunities, cash flow, *THE* crazy customer or that one email you forgot to send. And when that happens, you have two choices:

1. Toss and turn, getting frustrated.

2. Get your ass up and do something about it.

Now, I'm not saying sleepless nights are a badge of honor—your health always comes first. But let's be real: sometimes, the only way to shut your brain up is to get up and work. And honestly, there are some surprising advantages to working in the dead of night.

The Pros of Working at Night

Here's the thing about working at night: it's quiet. You're not getting bombarded by phone calls, emails, text messages, or employees knocking on your door with questions. It's just you and your thoughts, free of distractions. That kind of uninterrupted focus is rare during the day, and it's a golden opportunity to get shit done.

Some of my best ideas have come to me at 1 A.M. There's something about the stillness of the night that lets you think clearly. You can map out strategies, solve problems, or tackle that big project you've been avoiding. No one's expecting anything from you at midnight, so you're free to work on what matters most.

And let's not forget the satisfaction of going back to bed knowing you've knocked something important off your to-do list. It's like you've stolen a couple of bonus hours from the universe.

The Cons of Losing Sleep

Of course, there's a downside—because there's always a downside. Losing sleep isn't sustainable. If you're constantly burning the midnight oil, your productivity and decision-making will take a hit. Sleep deprivation messes with your memory, your mood, and your ability to focus. It's not just bad for your business; it's bad for your health.

There's also the risk of turning sleepless nights into a habit. One or two nights a month? Fine. But if you're pulling all-nighters every week, you're setting yourself up for burnout. And let me tell you, burnout is a one-way ticket to bad decisions, missed opportunities, and a whole lot of regret.

Finding the Balance

Here's how I see it: sleepless nights are part of the game, but they don't have to ruin you. The key is to make them work for you, not against you.

If you find yourself wide awake at night, don't waste time getting pissed off about it. Get up and tackle something meaningful. But set a limit. Work for an hour or two, then force yourself to get back to bed. You might not hit that magic eight hours of sleep, but you'll feel better knowing you turned your restlessness into productivity.

And don't forget to prioritize your health. Eat right, exercise, and make sleep a priority most nights. You can grind all you want, but if you're not taking care of yourself, your business will suffer in the long run.

The Bullshit of It All

The real bullshit here is that sleepless nights are inevitable, no matter how much you try to avoid them. As an entrepreneur, your mind is always going to be working overtime. That's just the nature of the beast.

But here's the good news: those sleepless nights don't have to be wasted. They can be an opportunity to get ahead, to solve problems, and to push your business forward. Just don't let them become the norm. There's no glory in running yourself into the ground.

So when you're lying there at 1 A.M., staring at the ceiling, ask yourself: "Will I feel better in the morning if I just get up and do something now?" If the answer is yes, then get up and make it happen. Because sometimes, the best way to deal with the bullshit is to embrace it.

Sweat equity is the most valuable equity there is. Know your business and industry better than anyone else in the world. Love what you do, or don't do it." **– Mark Cuban (Entrepreneur)**

Final Chapter 34: Wrapping It Up – The End of Business Bullshit
(But Just the Beginning for You)

Writing this book has been a lot of work, time and effort. It's forced me to revisit some of the messiest, most frustrating, and occasionally hilarious moments of my entrepreneurial journey. Honestly, it felt like therapy—except cheaper, with less awkward silence, and no one asking, "And how does that make you feel?"

But let's be clear about one thing: this book isn't about me. It's about you. Your journey. Your late nights questioning your sanity, your bold leaps of faith, and your battles with all the "business bullshit" that no one warns you about when you start.

The Thing About Business Bullshit

If there's one message I hope you take from this book, it's this: business doesn't have to be as complicated as people make it out to be. Sure, there's plenty of jargon, fluff, and "synergy" nonsense floating around, but at its core, business is pretty simple:

- Solve problems.

- Create value.

- Connect with people.

That's it. That's the game.

The rest? It's just noise. The endless meetings, the bloated processes, the corporate buzzwords—they're distractions. Real business is messy, unpredictable, and full of detours you never saw coming. But it's also rewarding, exciting, and—if you're lucky—fun.

Here's the truth: no one has it all figured out. Not me. Not the so-called "experts." Not even that person on LinkedIn who posts 17 times a day about how they're "crushing it." We're all just winging it, learning as we go, and hoping for the best. And that's okay.

Lessons I've Learned (the Hard Way)

If I could go back in time and give my younger self a pep talk, here's what I'd say:

1. Keep It Simple

Whether you're pitching an idea, designing a product, or writing an email, simplicity wins. Complexity might feel impressive, but clarity is what actually gets results.

2. Ask for Help

You don't have to do it all alone. Surround yourself with people who know things you don't, and don't be afraid to lean on them. Asking for help isn't a weakness—it's a strategy.

3. Laugh at Yourself

You're going to screw up. A lot. If you can't find the humor in your mistakes, this whole business thing is going to feel a lot harder than it needs to be.

4. Celebrate the Small Wins

The big milestones are great, but they're built on a million tiny victories. Don't wait for the "big moment" to celebrate—find joy in the progress you're making every day.

5. Remember Why You Started

So, What's Next for You?

Here's the exciting part: you get to decide.

Whether you're just starting out, expanding your business, or pivoting to something completely new, know this: you are capable, you are resilient, and you are absolutely going to figure it out.

Business isn't about having all the answers. It's about showing up, doing your best, learning as you go, persistence, resilience It's about progress—not perfection. And if you can approach it with a little humor and a lot of heart, you're already way ahead of the game.

The Real Ending

So, here we are. The end of "Business Bullshit." But for you, this is just the beginning.

Your journey will be full of challenges, surprises, and yes, plenty of bullshit. But it will also be full of growth, success, and moments of pride you can't even imagine yet.

Thank you for letting me be a part of your story, even in this small way. Now go out there, tackle the bullshit, and build something amazing. Because the only real "business bullshit" is believing you can't do it.

Remember always the three most important aspects of any business:

- Cash Flow – the lifeblood of the company
- Raving Customers – go the extra yard always, but especially with your first Five(5)
- Happy, intelligent employees with drive, good communication skills and analytic experience

You've got this.

Cheers to your success!

Please feel free to contact me with any questions or thoughts about this book.

Mike Ross, Author, Entrepreneur, Philanthropist

Mike@ConNEXTions.pro

818-823-3862

"Before you are a leader, success is all about growing yourself. When you become a leader, success is all about growing others." **- Jack Welch**

About the Author

Mike Ross' journey is one marked by an unyielding drive for excellence, both athletically and in the business realm. A recognized leader whose influence shapes national powerhouse companies and championship sports teams alike, Ross has earned a reputation for turning the dreams of organizations into tangible success. His legacy is etched in the lives he has shaped and the standards of excellence he has set in every arena he touches. Mike Ross exemplifies the spirit of a leader whose commitment extends far beyond the boardroom and the playing field.

Other Books by Mike Ross

Achieving Peace of Mind in Life, Business, and Sports

No Immediate Loyalty: Name, Image, Likeness: A Game-Changer in High School and College Sports

www.ingramcontent.com/pod-product-compliance
Lightning Source LLC
Chambersburg PA
CBHW071212210326
41597CB00016B/1781